THE CENTRAL SCHOOL OF SPEECH AND DRAMA

UNIVERSITY OF LONDON

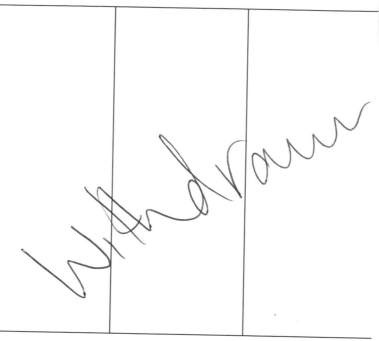

Please return or renew this item by the last date shown.

The Library, Central School of Speech and Drama,
Embassy Theatre, Eton Avenue, London, NW3 3HY
http://heritage.cssd.ac.uk
library@cssd.ac.uk
Direct line: 0207 559 3942

D0756339

3050971 8

Artists in the 1990s
Their Education and Values

ISSUES IN ART AND EDUCATION · VOLUME I

Papers submitted at conferences held at the Tate Gallery
in 1991 and 1992, organised by the Wimbledon School of Art
in collaboration with the Tate Gallery

Edited by Paul Hetherington
Department of History of Art and Contextual Studies
Wimbledon School of Art

WIMBLEDON SCHOOL OF ART

IN ASSOCIATION WITH

TATE GALLERY

Cover photograph by Rosie Potter

ISBN 1 85437 147 9
A catalogue record for this book is available from the British Library

Published by Tate Gallery Publications, London SW1P 4RG
© Wimbledon School of Art 1994 All rights reserved
Designed and typeset by Caroline Johnston
Printed in Great Britain by B.A.S. Printers Limited,
Over Wallop, Stockbridge, Hampshire

Contents

Acknowledgments

Neither the conferences nor this publication would have been possible without the generous support of a number of people. At the Tate Gallery our thanks are first due to the Director, Nicholas Serota, for making available the facilities of the Clore Gallery, and to the staff of the Education department, especially Richard Humphreys and Sylvia Lahav, for much essential assistance. In the Publications department the skilful care of Iain Bain and Judith Severne have seen this publication through the press. Finally, the energy and dedication of the office staff of Wimbledon School of Art, in particular Marie McCann, have been a *sine qua non* of the entire conference programme as well as this book.

Preface

CHRISTOPHER FRAYLING

Professor of Cultural History, The Royal College of Art

The joint Wimbledon School of Art/Tate Gallery conferences – on the teaching and practice of fine art, and the connections between them, in 1990s higher education – have rapidly become a key 'moment' in the academic calendar. Like degree shows and squabbles about whether painting involves 'research' or not, the conferences seem to have been around for ever and yet, amazing as it may seem, the first of these brave ventures happened as recently as 1991. I say brave, because the conferences have always dealt with debates and themes which are part of the great unspoken, the great taken-for-granted. A more usual response to these themes, by teachers and practitioners alike, has too often been 'let's be philosophical about this, don't give it a second thought', or 'don't think twice, it's alright!'

Themes such as: The role of the practitioner as teacher of fine art – does a gifted artist necessarily make a gifted teacher, and if so, what exactly is being taught? Can the demands of the curriculum and the demands of 'apprenticeship' sometimes be mutually exclusive? Is the practitioner–teacher concerned with teaching *to* art or teaching *through* art? (to re-use Herbert Read's famous distinction). These, and other related issues, formed the agenda for the first Wimbledon/Tate conference – and the quality of the ensuing debate amply demonstrated that contributors were delighted and relieved to have the opportunity to talk about them publicly. The second conference was about values in art, such as: Where do judgements about artistic value come from and by which criteria do teachers evaluate student work in the studios? What about the word 'value', which covers both commerce and ethics? At a time when the art market was booming (that meaning of 'value'), and the new art history had recently become the new orthodoxy (art as carrier of social values), this too, was a brave venture. And, if the debate was somewhat more diffuse than at the first conference, perhaps that reflected the nature of the theme.

I particularly remember the 'values' conference, because I'd just come back from the Valley of the Kings in Egypt, where I had been filming 'The Face of Tutankhamun' for the BBC, so such issues as cultural value, the role of history, Western values and 'orientalism', the glint of gold, were very much on my mind.

This publication brings together in one volume the proceedings of the first two Wimbledon School of Art/Tate Gallery conferences. Colin Painter of Wimbledon and Nicholas Serota of the Tate – together with their colleagues who made the events happen – deserve hearty congratulations. They've reminded us that – on the whole – it is much healthier to give it a second thought.

Introduction: A productive uncertainty

COLIN PAINTER

Principal, Wimbledon School of Art

Although the titles of the two conferences were expressed in positive form, they implicitly posed questions. First, who is best equipped to teach fine art in higher education? Second, what bases are there for making judgements of quality about fine art?

The contributors to the conferences were mainly, though not entirely, members of the fine art community; artists, teachers, critics, theoreticians. The response of this professional constituency to the two questions was coloured by the ways in which they originated within the world of higher education. The first, posed by a visiting panel in the context of a Council for National Academic Awards (CNAA) institutional review at Wimbledon School of Art, was taken to imply scepticism about the traditional role of the artist as teacher and was largely received as hostile. The resultant debate focused on the intrusion and impact of external and, in particular, political and resource-driven priorities on the teaching of fine art. The second question emerged from preoccupations within the discipline itself and generated a more clearly academic debate.

The origins of the first conference are sufficiently important to the nature of the papers to give an account of them. As an associated institution with the CNAA, the Wimbledon School of Art received its normal five yearly institutional review in 1990. The purpose of such events was that the CNAA should satisfy itself periodically that its associated institutions were fit places in which to offer courses culminating in its awards. Such events were much concerned with the notion of 'quality' – not only the quality of education itself, but of the processes by which quality was assured.

Wimbledon School of Art is one of the few remaining specialist art schools in England offering degree and postgraduate courses. Most other art schools are now faculties within the new universities. Such has been the pace of change in higher education that these universities were polytechnics at the time these conference papers were delivered and the CNAA itself has been closed. Processes of quality assessment and audit have been taken over by the Higher Education Funding Council for England (HEFCE) and the new Higher Education Quality Council (HEQC) respectively

The School presented itself to the CNAA visitors at the institutional review as a specialist institution committed to the education and training of professional artists and designers. In particular, we said, the School constitutes a community (staff and students) of practising artists and designers – with due acknowledgement made to the essential presence of scholars and academics in art history and related disciplines.

The teaching staff, it was explained, were all practitioners. Furthermore, half of them were part-time staff – professional artists and designers whose major commitment, at least in terms of time, was not to teaching but to painting, sculpture, design for theatre and so on. There was no separation for us between the worlds of fine art and theatre and the world of education towards those fields; though we did not see them as synonymous.

[11]

Perhaps most significantly, quality for us was mainly measured by reference to the readily available work of the students.

In the nicest possible way, the response of the visiting party was to ask how we knew all this was a good thing? In the report of the review we were specifically encouraged to explore the concept of the practitioner as teacher and to articulate it in relation to teaching and learning objectives. Perhaps with a little irritation, we accepted this as a legitimate suggestion. Questioning is so central to academic life that it is difficult to refute the obligation to respond thoughtfully to any question framed in a serious voice. It is, in any case, essential to higher education to stand outside one's taken for granted practices and observe them from a critical perspective – to question and examine orthodoxies.

We decided that any effective consideration of the value of using practising artists as teachers of fine art should be undertaken in conjunction with colleagues from outside the institution. A national conference with invited delegates to ensure a range of informed perspectives was planned. It was symptomatic of the School's understanding of itself as an extension of the fine art world that the Tate Gallery was chosen as the venue. With the notable exception of Glynn Williams, who was in charge of sculpture at Wimbledon when the event was planned, the speakers were drawn from outside the School. It was clear from the full attendance at the conference that the theme was of wide interest to the professional community of fine artists and art educators. It also became clear that this was because the particular circumstances that had given rise to the event struck a chord nationally.

To question the established role of the artist as teacher was perceived as symptomatic of a larger attack on the competence and authority of the professionals delivering art education. There was a sense that the agenda was not being defined in response to the demands of the discipline, but was being shaped from outside.

In a paper which offered a perspective on the recent history of art schools through his own education and subsequent teaching career in higher education, Glynn Williams argued that the agenda was increasingly determined by an unsympathetic management primarily concerned with achieving and justifying cuts in resources. In particular, he complained that this had resulted in the loss of part-time staff who provided the indispensable presence of practising artists.

There were different views expressed on the subject of the tenure of part-time staff. Glynn Williams regretted that they had often been the first to go when financial cuts were being made and argued that they should have security of tenure. Clive Ashwin, on the other hand, expressed the view that it was largely the capacity to change part-time staff that made them such a valuable resource, bringing the most current insights and perspectives in contact with students. Williams considered that reductions in resources and the reduced presence of artists as teachers were resulting in a decline in the quality of fine art education nationally, but that this decline was not being adequately registered.

It is significant that the funding methodology (which at the time of the conference was organised by the PCFC) included a method of financially rewarding high quality in institutions. While this might be justifiable in itself, it has, in effect, constituted a systematic deterrent to institutions against declaring that their quality might be dropping.

Such a declaration would, in any case, be detrimental to recruitment. No loss of quality is likely to emerge from examination results, since the procedures and traditions associated with examining in higher education tend to reproduce similar results in relation to an unexpressed assumption of 'normal distribution'. Academics would, in any case, avoid visiting the consequences of financial cuts upon the students who have enrolled on degree courses in good faith. This is not to imply that this would be consciously implemented as policy but that it would be likely to allow a gradual process of decline.

For various reasons, therefore, the government is able to claim an increase in student numbers and no loss of quality. In addition to muffling evidence of falling quality, should it exist, the commercial and competitive model now operative in higher education is in danger of undermining academic exchange and openness – as well as the valuable tradition of objective peer group review established by the CNAA and now, to some extent, continuing in the quality audit procedures of the HEQC and in the quality assessment procedures of the HEFCE. It is becoming increasingly problematic to expect academic staff from institutions competing in the commercial market place to exchange critical views and information in an open and detached way. Would it be reasonable, in the commercial world, to expect the managing director of one company to pass neutral and detached judgement on the practices and products of a rival dealing in the same product? If that would be reasonable, would it be reasonable to expect the managing director of the rival to accept the judgement as detached and neutral? In a commercially competitive education system academic and educational advances can be expected to become closely guarded and art and design is particularly vulnerable since debate and exchange – the free flow of ideas – are central to it.

Government-imposed resource constraints are more or less common to all disciplines and, once imposed, simply have to be coped with. But it is presumably important to be able to distinguish between the introduction of resource-driven educational measures as necessary expedients and their advocacy as valuable pedagogic advancements. Andrew Brighton, in particular, argued that this distinction has been obscured and that pedagogic theory, as well as the rhetoric of quality assurance processes, has been permeated and distorted by underlying economic imperatives.

There is no doubt that a few years ago, a CNAA visiting party asking about a staff/student ratio (SSR) would want to hear that there were plenty of staff in relation to numbers of students. By the time the CNAA closed, the reverse was the case. If you had a lot of staff, inefficiency was likely to be implied and you would, at least, be asked to show that you had adequate contingency plans to cope without them. It is common now to hear educational managers talking of achieving a 'better' SSR, meaning that there are fewer members of staff per student. This reversal is often supported by the argument that students are 'over-taught', that what is important is that students should take responsibility for their own learning; independent learning is advocated. But good teaching methodology has always embodied these concepts and having plenty of staff to support students has also been considered valuable. These are not alternatives but should go hand in hand. Of course, it is possible to over-teach and to fail to put the student's learning experience at the centre. Along with other disciplines fine art has been guilty of this. The obvious cure is not to reduce staff numbers.

Faced with insurmountable external resource constraints 'making do' is inevitable. But unless we are clear that that is what is happening – the concept of quality will become meaningless. It is, of course, through quality assurance and control procedures that educational quality should be most clearly under scrutiny. But there were doubts expressed at the conference about the effectiveness of such procedures in fine art as currently carried out nationally. As exemplified in the last days of the CNAA and in the degree awarding new universities, the procedures increasingly aspire to address issues of educational quality more or less independently of particular disciplines. Questions are raised as though they have universal validity across disciplines and educationists from outside a particular discipline are increasingly involved in the discussion of quality issues within it.

While this can be profitable it has, as Glynn Williams pointed out, resulted in the work of the individual students in fine art being given less importance as an indicator of the quality of teaching and learning. This is very largely because the people carrying out the quality assessment are not equipped to make the necessary judgements. Andrew Brighton maintained that the expectations of what he called 'the scrutineers' are often antipathetic to essential characteristics of the discipline – for example the expectation that fine art criteria for assessment should be made explicit. In his view fine art is characterised by complexity and debate – inherently incommensurable with the rational discourse of management which now dominates quality assurance processes. He complains that art education is reshaping itself for the scrutineers with indifference to its own educational character.

There was also considerable debate about the extent to which fine artists could reasonably be expected to be explicit about what they were doing. Some felt that to attempt to explain was always reductive if not destructive. Others considered this to be mystification and recognised the obligation to articulate the priorities of the discipline. Had there been an opportunity to explore this further, it might have resolved itself more clearly into disagreement about the level of analysis and specificity of description that was possible rather than a disagreement about the principle. Distinctions would probably also have emerged between aspects that could reasonably be made explicit and aspects which could not.

As the Registrar for Art and Design at the CNAA, Judith Chaney had the unenviable task of presenting the perspective of the non-specialist 'scrutineer'. She felt that the speakers at the conference had not addressed what she saw as the key issue implied by the conference theme – the distinctiveness of the contribution made by artists as teachers. In this she was correct and underlined a central fact that had determined the nature of the discussion – that the scepticism underlying the question of the role of artists as teachers came from outside the paradigm. For those within fine art education the implicit issue in the conference theme was the very fact that such a silly and dangerous question should be on the agenda. For them the answer to the question of why artists are the right people to teach student artists was so obvious that it did not need to be articulated – and that is that artists know best about the skills and knowledges associated with being artists. Of course, they also need to be good teachers – it is not a sufficient condition to be an artist but it is an essential one. Central to this is the associated assumption that good fine art education manifested itself in good work produced by students and that this judgement of quality was most appropriately made by artists engaged in like activity.

Participating as an educationist from outside art and design, John Cowan talked most directly of teaching methods and theory and provided a model of experiential learning. He considered that art education was, in fact, particularly good at implementing the model by comparison with many other disciplines. From the perspective of the artist/teacher, Jon Thompson approached pedagogic theory by asserting the essential importance of 'desire'. This could be said to characterise attitudes to the educational process in art schools where elaborated pedagogic theory has little currency and the learning process tends to be a taken for granted product of a passion for the subject. Education in the art schools makes little reference to the body of educational theory related, for example, to psychology and the processes of learning. While the theory of art education in the UK has a distinguished literature, it has mainly informed primary and secondary education (and the world of teacher education) and received little attention within fine art in higher education, where the literature of art education tends to be the literature of art itself. There were delegates at the conference who considered that this lack of engagement with pedagogy was actually a virtue and Glynn Williams juxtaposed educationists and artists as figures with opposing interests.

Perhaps it is possible to argue that pedagogic theory – construed as the theory of facilitating learning – is less necessary (though not unnecessary) where the student brings to the learning situation an existing and passionate commitment. Arguably, it is most necessary where the student is least ready to learn. Higher education, and fine art education in particular, has tended to assume an existing commitment in the student to the educational enterprise. This cannot, however, be taken to mean that sound teaching methodology will not enhance the learning process for committed students. Furthermore, with the current expansion in higher education and the development of broad-based and modular fine art courses – or courses in which fine art is only a part – 'passion' from the student might not be so confidently assumed. This was, itself, a matter of concern at the conference as was the extent to which the essential characteristics of fine art education could be sustained in non-specialist courses.

The second conference, which explored bases for making judgements of value about art, concentrated more clearly on academic and pedagogic issues. This seemed to be because the theme was not, in itself, seen as contentious. It was an expression of an existing acceptance within the art world that how art, and the achievements of art students, was evaluated was not 'written in tablets of stone' but was properly the subject of debate.

The papers from this second conference threw a great deal of light on the matters raised in the first. Particularly significant was a more or less shared commitment to fine art as the location of a debate about values where little could be assumed to have the authority of certainty. It lent support to Andrew Brighton's view, expressed at the first conference, that what he saw as the scrutineer's search for certainty was inappropriate.

The acknowledgement of the contentious nature of value judgements about fine art did not imply for any of the speakers that judgements could not be meaningfully made. The philosopher Anthony O'Hear attempted to rescue aesthetic judgements from the purely subjective domain. In a closely argued paper he offered the possibility that aesthetic judgements, though based in human response, relate to real characteristics of things in the external world. He suggested that 'the aesthetic might be a realm of objective value'.

Both Michael Ginsborg and Paul Huxley, as practising artist/teachers, conveyed the complexity of the situation for those aware of the vastness of the theoretical terrain, having to purposefully engage with the individual aspirations of students. Both implied that the basis for making value judgements about art should be looked for in the logic of the artist's approach to the business of painting. Huxley suggests that 'ideally' the work of art itself should reveal to the spectator how it should be read. But with an admirable absence of dogma he discusses his way from that position, via the possibility that 'grappling with the puzzle' might be integral, to a final note of apparent doubt about the possibility of congruence between the meaning grasped by the spectator and that 'intended' in the work. This ultimate agnosticism is not despairing but relishes the uncertainty and is held within a larger conviction that 'art not only can be taught but must be taught'.

Perhaps, within this paradigm, the doubt is the discipline. Perhaps fine art can be evaluated by reference to the extent to which it generates doubt. Perhaps one reason that it is essential that artists do the teaching is that they know and value this doubt and can share it authentically – fine art as essentially a debate about the variable nature of experience and the meanings of representations. There would seem to be no reason why doubt and debate should not themselves be operationalised in curricula and evidenced through assessment criteria.

Ginsborg identifies two major emphases in current artistic practice, each implying values against which to make judgements about art. On the one hand there is a commitment to art as critical discourse addressing political and ideological issues, including the deconstruction of art as an institution; on the other there is a commitment to 'the eye', to intuition, spontaneity, discovery and search – perhaps for the self. He believes that the second emphasis is dominant in art schools and that it is often unmediated by discourse because of the gulf that exists between theory and practice. This can result in students engaging in the studios in untheorised individual expression which, though inevitably rooted in historical traditions and received conventions, tends to be evaluated simply in relation to notions of individuality and originality. Being unaware of the way in which their practices are situated and not having had to theorise them they can find themselves later in life wondering what they are doing. In the terms of the conference theme this is perhaps another way of saying that, when unsupported by the art school context, students have no way of evaluating their activity or its products.

Ana Maria Pacheco offered a very personal paper which resonates convincingly of the particular nature of her work as an artist. She gives emphasis to cultural influences in shaping meaning and value in art and gives more than a hint of a commitment to a moral (at least 'humanist') dimension. This would appear to be discordant with Marjorie Allthorpe Guyton's support for the traditional distinction between art and life. The final statement in her paper is that 'art must be amoral – its assertions neither sacred nor profane'. Quoting Duchamp, she seems resigned to the possibility that the concerns of art may be elitist and confined to an initiated few.

The social location of fine art was implicitly, if not explicitly, addressed by Rachel Mason who, as a 'teacher trainer' is engaged in the preparation of teachers who will work in primary and secondary schools where a National Curriculum has recently been established ensuring the continued teaching of art to all children, at least up to the age of thirteen years. Rachel Mason's contribution was important in drawing attention to the fact that fine art in higher education is part of a wider educational system and fine artists are part of a wider social fabric. The social location and relevance of fine art may not be quite the hot issue that it was in Britain in the late 1960s and 1970s, but it remains problematic in the context of art education. An educational discipline in a democratic society where education is supported from general taxation is in a dangerous position (not to mention a morally questionable one) if it does not appear useful to the people who might study it and are expected to pay for it.

Rachel Mason's paper gives an account of her own art school experience where she was taught by 'distinguished' artists who, she feels, had not made explicit the relativity and historical particularity of their artistic persuasions. It is an account that would have been valuable at the first conference and it is interesting to be able to read it here in relation to the papers from the earlier event. It represents a persuasive argument for the importance of pedagogic awareness, if not training, among artists engaged in teaching.

Mason finished her paper by asserting the conviction that art can be evaluated when evaluation is carried out by 'connoisseurs'. By connoisseurs she means people with a trained perception and experience in the field. Neither she nor the larger conference gave much attention to the definition of 'the field' of fine art within the larger social and cultural context.

The values, priorities, modes of response and perception central to higher education in fine art co-exist with different value systems outside the professional culture itself. It is a mistake to assume that fine art is the visual culture in the UK and that people are either sensitive to it or not. Image making and the uses of images take a number of forms in Britain within the indigenous population as well as, more obviously, among minority ethnic groups. More attention needs to be given to the fact that the professional culture of fine art (as represented in art schools) is in interaction with other image cultures or, if you like, art worlds – though the word 'art' is not appropriate since the way in which many people use images in our society has little to do with, and actually rejects association with, the concept of 'art'. In relation to the first conference this raises the fundamental question of how we identify the 'artist' in the notion of the 'artist as teacher'. The answer would seem to be that, for the purposes of the conference, the term 'artist' was taken to denote the practitioner as broadly construed within the current professional and scholarly fine art establishment, producing work as institutionalised in the official collections of contemporary fine art. This conception of the artist (this 'professional culture') is associated with a particular and selective historical tradition. It co-exists in the UK with other conceptions.

In this cultural co-existence it is necessary to give realistic reasons for claiming a special status for fine art which justifies its place in education. No one culture can claim superiority in a general sense. It is necessary to identify the things that the tradition of image making associated with fine art can achieve and argue the value of these for people generally. One sport cannot be said to be intrinsically superior to another (though sport is not free from cultural politics) but it is legitimate to argue that one sport is more effective than another in developing strength whilst another is superior in developing speed. The cuisine of one culture cannot be claimed intrinsically superior to another but one may legitimately be claimed more nutritious than another. In such specific respects it is legitimate to claim the superiority of one sport or diet over another. It still remains to be argued whether we should value nutrition over sugariness, muscular strength over speed. We know this clearly when considering the different manifestations of 'art' across history and across international cultures. We lose sight of it within our own social and cultural diversity.

Fortunately there is no obligation in this essay to attempt a definition of the special-ness of the recent dominant fine art tradition which makes it essential to higher educa-tion but, collectively, the papers contained in this volume would appear to support the idea that the countenance of doubt, debate and uncertainty is central.

The Artist as Teacher

Chairman's Introduction to
the First Conference

CHRISTOPHER FRAYLING

Professor of Cultural History, The Royal College of Art

Welcome to this one day Conference organised by Wimbledon School of Art at the Tate Gallery: 'The Artist as Teacher'. The conference will be approaching this important and very timely topic from a variety of perspectives: that of the professional artist, the educationalist, the cultural theorist, the administrator, the historian and of course the teacher.

A few years ago I wrote a book about the history of art education in Britain, which now nestles side by side with Clive Ashwin's volume on documents in art education. In the course of researching it I came across three stories which for me epitomise the basic theme of this conference.

The first dates from the 1880s, when Princess Louise, who was Queen Victoria's daughter, applied to go to the South Kensington School to study sculpture. Until this time she had been taught entirely by Palace tutors who had been vetted by Queen Victoria. The night before she arrived in South Kensington to start her sculpture career as a student, Queen Victoria wrote her a letter of advice which contains the deathless phrase 'you must be awfully careful of "Fine Artists" my dear, you can never be quite sure where they have been'. Clearly where the Palace was concerned, the professional teacher was in some way respectable and the professional artist in some way was not. The person who combines the two was decidedly suspect. Needless to say Princess Louise came to the college, subsequently became a sculptress of sorts, and founded the equivalent of the CNAA in Canada.

The second story dates from the 1960s and concerns a recently appointed visiting professor, who was also a major artist. He wrote home to his mother telling her the great news about his appointment. She wrote back to him immediately saying how thrilled she was, after all he hadn't got any O Levels or A Levels and had left school at sixteen, and how terrific it was that he should have become a Professor and by the way the word had one 'f' and two 's's.

The question of the social and intellectual status of artists as teachers has been something that has obsessed British art education for most of this century and I believe that it is part of the theme of today as well. Not that you spell professor with two 'f's but what the hell does it matter?

The third story dates from the early 1960s, when in the Painting School at the Royal College a lecturer in aesthetic theory from Oxford University came to give a series of four lectures to the painting students. He hadn't really been told about what sort of lectures they might expect so he arrived with beautiful typescript, lots of footnotes, obscure references to texts in German, and no slides. At his first lecture all the students were there – a total of about twenty-five. At his second there were five. At his third lecture there were two students and at his final lecture there was one solitary student. It is said to have been David Hockney. The professor of aesthetics turned to the solitary student and said 'there's not much point going on with the lecture, why don't we just chat about it over a cup of coffee?' To this the student replied 'I do wish you would go on, I've been trying to draw you for four weeks'.

The great gulf between what we call theory – our philosopher of art – and what we call practice – our solitary art student sitting there drawing – is a gulf which is I believe actually programmed into the British system of higher education in art, and has been for the last thirty years. Obviously this is part of the theme of this conference as well. It is actually remarkable, that of the most significant modern experiments in art and design education, the Bauhaus in Germany lasted for about twelve years, the Hochschule at Ulm in its pure form lasted for seven years and the Coldstream reforms (reforms which, as Jon Thompson has pointed out, put easel painting Slade style at the centre of the studio and history Courtauld style everywhere else, which definitively put a separation between doers and scholars) have just celebrated their thirtieth birthday. Not that anyone noticed this event or indeed if they had, not that the system had enough puff left to blow out the candles. Thirty years is a very long time for an experiment in art education. Some, including me, would argue much too long.

A hundred years ago, when Princess Louise was still struggling to find out what fine artists really do, this basic distinction between the 'practitioner' and the 'theorist' would probably not even have been recognised. It is an invention of the late nineteenthth century. Design thinking and art thinking lay at the root of design doing and art doing and teachers of both persuasions I believe, certainly from my researches, tried to communicate both the grammar and the usage as best they could. There was no concept of 'you do the grammar and I'll do the usage'. You did both at once. But then again when Princess Louise was around words like 'creative' and 'original' and 'individual' and 'challenging' had not yet become part of the educational vocabulary either. So perhaps there is a lesson there for today. Anyway, today the implications of the theme 'The Artist as Teacher' are as wide ranging and as significant as ever.

What exactly is the relationship between student and artist? A relationship of apprenticeship, of sharing good practice, of example, of emulation, of identification, or peer group criticism, or what exactly? Why are the artists who are full-time teachers protected by all concerned more than the artists who are part-time teachers? If the artists become career teachers does this in some way diminish them, and in whose eyes? What is actually being taught in the studios or is teaching not quite the right word for what goes on? Why is the romantic model of the artist still so pervasive when art institutions themselves have become less and less romantic places, to say the least. Above all, perhaps the most basic question for this conference: do you have to be an artist in order to teach other artists, and if so why?

Piloting through these incredibly dangerous waters is a remarkable group of speakers. I think it is a great tribute to Colin Painter to have got them all together; I've never seen such a good line-up on this subject, and they will be approaching the theme from a variety of points of view.

The practitioner, once a ubiquitous presence in art and design education, is now a rarity: A history of the blooming and decline of the species

GLYNN WILLIAMS

Professor of Sculpture, The Royal College of Art

This brief paper only allows me to make my points in very black and white terms. This will appear over-simplified to many, but should at least allow the issues to be seen clearly.

I have always had the simplistic view that in art education the student worked as near to the artist as possible. If you are educating towards the highest attainments of the professional practice, then the presence of the practitioner goes without saying. Or does it? It now appears not. Some educationalists now see the practitioners as inept, exclusive, irresponsible – even dangerous – as distributors of knowledge.

I am only going to discuss undergraduate education as it is over this area that the question seems to hang. I can only talk about fine art, and in that area I would like to give a very brief potted history of the last thirty years, of the introduction, spread and now decline of the practitioner as teacher.

Until the early 1960s, nearly every town in the country had its own art school and there were well over two hundred of them. They taught their students a national curriculum under the syllabus of the National Diploma in Art and Design. With a few very notable exceptions, the teachers were one-time artists who had ceased to practice regularly, or teachers who had never practised on a professional level. The criteria for national assessment were based upon traditional attitudes to craft-skill, ability and basic formal aesthetics. Under this system, the individual student's creative and inventive achievement was impossible to attend to on any appropriate level. It is now quite startling to recall that, despite what the contemporary art world was doing, Victorian academic values were what most art schools taught their students, right up until 1963. There was a national art education of repetition and stasis.

Obviously there was pressure for this to change, and in the early 1960s the system was completely overturned and at last modern art, its attitudes and its practice took over its own education. The next ten years saw the old NDD go through a further Diploma stage, and end up as a university equivalent honours degree, with its courses, for the most part, now forced into the new polytechnics. As in all changes, it could be argued that some things of value may have been lost, but the education did now approach and acknowledge the reality of the practice.

The significant fact about those years was that professional artists – the practitioners – were in evidence in increasing numbers, as teachers and assessors on courses, and

[23]

later, sitting as panel members on national validating committees and financing bodies. The practitioner – and more often, the younger practitioner – was a dominant presence in art education. When I finally finished as a student in 1964, it was possible to get a part-time teaching job in almost any art school. There was almost an unspoken form of state sponsorship for the young artist. And the pre-requisite, that applicants must practice, accompanied every advertised teaching post. To be allowed to run these new courses, art schools had to be vetted. This was done by specialist teams, that were heavily weighted with practitioners. One of the criteria used was the quantity of practitioner input that a course had. At the end of this exercise there were fewer than fifty art schools allowed to offer courses at this new level.

All art schools desperately wanted the reality of the relevant contemporary art world in their institutions, if not for their own reasons, then for those of the validating panels. The price that they had to pay for this was to listen and bend to the views of the expert professional – which although new and exciting for the student, often seemed idiosyncratic and sometimes insulting to long-held opinions of the existing staff. However, the pay-off was a world-leading art education, internationally recognised. Its aspiration was the highest attainable quality for the student work, based upon examples set by the best the art world could offer – and its teachers were the best practitioners that the individual schools could attract. For the first time, the contemporary evolution in art could be seen reflected in the studios of the art schools. And most importantly, the work of the individual student was attended to, compared and assessed in terms of its own quality by appropriate artist/teachers. The practitioners brought a sense of real comparison in quality between the individual student's work and the art world beyond the art school walls. The student became a true student of art, aspiring towards its practice and inspired by its practitioners. Undergraduate fine art education at many art schools was truly of a postgraduate level, based as it was on encouraging original perception and research, rather than the prescribed achievement of known ends. A lot of money was put into the system and it moved away from other subject areas of higher education in its maturity and relevance to its subject. It was often accused of being elitist, but it was undeniably the best art education that existed anywhere.

The last ten years have been a steady decline in both provision and quality of provision, the main factors in this decline being:

a) a reducing financial input;
b) untenured part-time teaching;
c) a polarising of attitudes between the practitioner and the educator;
d) a growing over-flexibility towards the subject taught;
e) individual short-sighted intrigue and manoeuvring, based upon political and economic expediency.

The financial constraints have steadily tightened over the last fifteen years, and continue to do so. They lie behind everything else and all later developments and changes, however packaged, have been answers to a diminishing resource. With few exceptions, the practitioners never risked their professional work by taking on full-time posts. In those heady days of the late 1960s and early 1970s there seemed no need to worry, that, officially, the part-time teacher had absolutely no security. Rather than seeing security for the part-timers, as being just of benefit to that individual, the institutions should have realised the greater benefit to themselves, of this, their richest asset. When cuts came, the easiest and superficially, the most economic thing to lose, was the unsecured part-time teacher. As far as administrating authorities went, these were but numbers of allocated hours. During those years, several younger practitioners matured into established members of their institutions, even moving away from student contact and climbing into top management. Their jobs were secure but they no longer practised their art at a professional level, and their creativity now found an outlet in committee politics and organisation. Not only did they cease to provide a practitioner input, some were also party to expedient moves to reduce the presence of other practitioners.

For years the voice of the practitioner had been the accepted form of relevance, bringing the reality of an outside aspiration of the highest level into the art school. The practitioner was the guardian of quality. Gradually the administrators and organisers found that their creative schemes for expedient educational changes were better not challenged by the qualitative view of these independent spirits. And with great shows of sadness they let them go. Likewise, the committees running our national system of art education, which ten years earlier were filled with specialist practitioners as advisers, now were reduced to a token membership.

The practitioners' opinion of their own subject was the expert voice of authority, and this was inconvenient to those trying to change courses according to expedient financial and educational ends. So, the great 'moving of the goalposts' began. In fine art the subjects were shuffled around, mingled, interbred, until various hybrids emerged as unqualifiable pluralistic activities that had their reality only inside education. As their experts they now had their educational creators – they were no longer governed by the realities of a subject and no longer needed the practitioners. Art education that abandons its subject for some fashionable educational self-reliance, will isolate its students in the unreal and unrelated void of institutionalised impotence. They will become the ideal environment for the art 'theorist' to flourish, toying with the fundamentals of the subject without responsibility of the practice.

Can education be a self-referring practice in its own right? At the level that I'm talking about in art, I don't think it can. The art student wishing to study painting or sculpture is researching and experiencing a subject that has a real existence. They are joining an age-old activity that is ongoing and has its reality outside the walls of the educational institution. To involve the student's own practice as aspiring artist, the course can only have benefit if its aim is to join its subject at the highest point of its 'front-line' activity.

Knowledge of the past is implicit in any idea of progress or originality. To wish to alter or change existing perception assumes a full knowledge of the past, but with some form of dissatisfaction with it, and this is the motor that enables the student to go beyond simply repeating what has already been. A challenge to existing perceptions can only have relevance when it is linked through knowledge to the past, but the past as a reality and not just a theory. A subject such as painting or sculpture comprises of its history, interdependent with its current perception and its formative and vulnerable future. The subject cannot exist without reference to its practitioners. An education in the subject can only be valid if it reflects the reality of that subject and the best messengers of that reality are the practitioners.

In the recent past, when government bodies asked undergraduate fine art courses to change to a more general, pluralistic stance, with a greater range of access and more evident transferable skills, etc., those involved who were practitioners had simply to refer to their subject. If one were teaching sculpture, say, then it was sculpture that provided the aims and objectives, outlined the syllabus and defined the quality of what was acceptable. Those involved who were educators saw it as an opportunity of wresting the education away from the reality of the practice and claiming it in its newly created form as an end in itself. The recent abolition of separate subjects of study in many fine art courses, although in the guise of a creative change, has caused the rampant destruction of previously strong courses and been used to remove many specialist practitioners.

A little while ago we in art education could, and should, have hung our heads, realising that we only had ourselves to blame for what was happening to the quality of the education. Now that blame has been assimilated and laundered, and quite suddenly nothing is wrong, there are good educational reasons that state that what we mistook for a decline, should be seen as an improvement. As a vindication of what, earlier, would have been completely indefensible, there arose the first murmurings of criticism towards the practitioner's presence as teacher. Educational ineptitude, bias and irresponsibility were more than hinted at. These murmurings grew into stronger outbursts and were eventually written down in papers on teaching and learning methods, and appeared as agenda items on committees, and on checklists of what validating bodies expected of institutional self-appraisal. Suddenly it's open season on the practitioner.

Assessing and discussing quality in individual student products has become unfashionable and is avoided, because those most able to do this task are the practitioners. But the practitioners stand accused of bias, subjective opinion and unclear explanations of their criteria. As a result it is being assumed by many that qualitative assessment of the art product is pointless, as it represents only unreliable individual taste. The alternative to looking at the quality in individual work is to look at the quality of the 'learning context' – its methods and monitoring. This allows the educator, rather than the practitioner, to become the expert. Systems and mechanisms that monitor the 'learning context' will be assessed, rather than the individual student product. For the student this will remove the obvious and essential role of 'comparison' with art work outside the educational context and in the reality of the subject.

It may be that occasionally, different artists have differing views about attitudes to student work; of course they will. These are seen by the student in the context of those individual artists' work, background and endeavour, and have a reality that is appropriate to the knowledge needed to progress. This is what the students learn for themselves about their own work when put into contact with the bias of the practitioner. They will know that a similar qualitative knowledge of their own history and particular direction is a necessity that has to be struggled with before a maturity can appear in their own work.

I believe that any system which puts the maximum number of relevant artists as close to the student as possible, with the intention of attending to that student's work in the context of its declared subject, will always be a good one, no matter how it is run. We have had such a system, but to try to return to it now would require the transfer of allocated resources away from management and back to the studio floor with the students. However, we are in a climate of further education corporations with administrative, financial and marketing management, where the running of the institution is where the maximum resource is targeted.

Over the last twelve months we continually read of pay negotiations where art teachers can, for a percentage pay rise, sell their old practitioner's soul to the director of their polytechnic. It is obvious that the last remnants of the practitioner whose teaching/practice was such a careful balance is bound to disappear.

There is a diagrammatic law describing the inevitable escalation for success or decline, from high plateau to low, or vice versa. The more 'objectors to change' that are removed, the faster will be the change and the easier will be the removal of any remaining objections. According to the theory, this escalation cannot be stopped until it achieves its own objective, and flattens again into stasis.

Rather than practitioners, who were the guardians of quality in the individual student work, courses now have elaborate quality control systems and committees. They sift opinions, diagnose activity, canvas views, monitor development – all minuted and recorded. They take a lot of people's time and effort. But as they grow and develop, so their increased resourcing diminishes that available for the traditional staff/student contact – and so standards in the actual work of the student falls. The sadness is that this decline in standards (which I have observed in many courses around the country) is not being picked up by the system that is set up to monitor it. If the system works smoothly, if its information is coming in and going out, if its participants all have their proper say, if it meets regularly and everything is duly recorded, then the system sees itself as working – and all is well. But who is actually standing in front of the student's work and assessing its quality, assisting its evolution and progress, and helping the student build a reliable ruler of quality for themselves? Certainly fewer and fewer people who would seem likely to be able to do so.

Let me give you my deliberately grim prediction. Instead of the old national curriculum of thirty years ago, we could soon have a national system of quality appraisal appearing to work smoothly, but once more incapable of attending to the individual expectations of the student's creative work in relationship to the current reality of their subject. As money is taken away from art education, or diverted from student/teacher contact, then the standard of the product of that education will fall, and the first to sound a warning should be the practitioner – except, now on a national level, there may be too few to be heard.

How can students of art and design best be helped to learn and develop?

JOHN COWAN

The Open University, Scotland

Introduction

I was the person who asked the question 'How do you know how good you are?' during the CNAA visit to Wimbledon. There is something delightfully Machiavellian about having been asked to help Wimbledon to answer it.

I became an educational manager about three and a half years ago: my paper is thus given as an educationist. I was in practice as a structural engineer for longer than I have been an educationalist; and I was a teacher for longer than I was an educationist. So I still think of the predominant part of my background as being 'in practice'. I'm conscious, though, of presenting this paper with the label of an educationist. Now, to some extent there is a feeling in higher education that professionals built the *Titanic* but amateurs built the Ark. Perhaps there is a feeling that amateurs are better at a lot of things, especially in education, than professionals. That may be true; but the people who built the Ark *did* have their limitations. For example, Noah was the first bureaucrat; he insisted in filing everything in duplicate. And maybe the amateurs who engage in education have limitations as well. So I intend to look at our present practices in teaching in the creative area, in relation to the pedagogy of adult learning, in as professional a manner as possible.

In doing so, I will try to remember Thurber's story about the wee girl who had been asked, with the other children in her class, to read a book about penguins and then write an essay about it. Her essay was one sentence long. It just said 'This book told me more about penguins than I wanted to know'. I'll try not to tell you more about the pedagogy of adult learning than you would wish to know.

We will start from what is known about adult learning; interestingly, much of what I'm summarising as good practice is exemplified better in many schools of art and design, in my experience, than in departments of engineering.

A Model of Learning

What, then, do we know about the way adults learn? I'm not really very interested in learning which only covers acquiring knowledge and understanding. I think these are fairly basic educational objectives, achieved in an instructional type of teaching and learning situation. I'm more concerned with higher level abilities, and with those factors which relate to what people call 'experiential learning'.

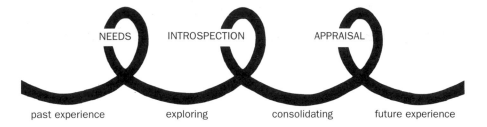

The diagram above is a revision of a diagram produced by a man called Kolb, about experiential learning. I hope this is a little more informative than the original; I believe it says more about what we know from researches into the way adults learn.

Adults bring past experience with them into learning situations. In bringing that past experience with them, they will learn most effectively if they have some kind of motivation. That motivation comes because they identify needs or aspirations or desires to move in a certain direction. An analogy portrays the learner as an aeroplane, looping the loop. As the learner progresses from left to right, we have experience and development; and as the learner loops, we have reflection on what has been going on, or what is going to happen. So the first factor that is going to lead to effective learning is that there is a conscious reflection on experience (first loop): 'Where is it that I want to go, and how will I know when I've got there, even if my target is an interim target?' The looping takes a relatively short time.

The next thing that happens in good experiential learning is an exploratory experience. A student once asked me: 'John, do you play the bagpipes?' I said 'No'. He said 'Well, if I were going to teach you to play the bagpipes, I would give you this thing that looks like an octopus and would then find an excuse to go away for ten minutes or so. I would let you discover if you could blow up the bag and if you could balance it on your arm without it falling off or attacking you. If you could manage to squeeze the bag so that you could get some noises out of it, then you would know what you wanted me to help you with first. I would come back and you would tell me what you wanted to know we would start from there.'

In anything which involves experiential learning, we should be arranging what students should think of as 'throw-away' experiences, which are exploratory yet in which where they discover more meaningfully through actually being involved in the new experience, what it is that they want to learn and that they need to learn; and particularly what it is that they want to concentrate on first. That experience will be more fruitful if we follow it with the second loop of reflection in which the students look back over these exploratory experiences and say 'Now I know what I want you to concentrate on first'; and if they look forward into the next surge of experiences and say, 'And I also know where I need to consolidate, where I need to develop my learning'. So the second experience we plan for them as teachers is very different from the first; because the purpose of the first experience was to allow learners, in an unthreatened, way to explore, experiment, make mistakes and learn from those mistakes. But the purpose of the second experience is to consolidate and advance the learning, though without necessarily completing it.

The last reflective loop is the one in which you take stock, and say 'Right, I've made some progress there; but I have lots of other items on my agenda. Have I made enough progress that I am ready to carry this out into future experiences and deal for the meantime with certain other items in my agenda?'

Implications

If that is our model of how adults learn, then I am suggesting that there are five significant features to be read into it.

First, the model calls for there to be more than one similar experience. The exploratory experience is developed in the consolidation. There are too many cases where we teach based on experience and where the students only have one experience, which either has to be exploratory or consolidating or a hopeless amalgam of both. The first feature that I would look for in effective experiential learning would be a developing sequence of at least two experiences. (There is nothing in the model that precludes a number of intermediate loops before we get to the last reflective loop).

The second feature which is important is the role of reflection. In many of the creative experiences that students engage in, certainly in engineering, there is a feeling abroad that if we just let them do something – engage in projects, or design – then they will get better. There has been some salutary research on golfers which has discovered that, on average, if a golfer practices he or she gets slightly worse: repeated experiences can contribute to a deterioration in performance. What contributes to the purposeful improvement in performance is if the golfer, in between experiences, stops and says 'I wonder why seven of the last eight balls that I've hit have curved round like that; and I wonder what I might change to stop that happening?' That is what Donald Schon calls a reflection on action or reflection in action – a brief reflection in the midst of what we are doing that tends to lead to the improvement and development. It's not a reflection on where the eight balls went, but a reflection on what might be changed, which makes the performance better. There is thus a key role for reflection in experiential learning.

The third feature is that this describes a model of learning, and therefore a model of teaching, in which it is not significant, nor useful, to tell someone what to do. *You* can't have experiences for *me*. What a teacher can do for me is to accelerate the process of my learning from experience, because it has been structured so that I don't have to rediscover the wheel. But even if there are experiences that people learn from, then I must still have these experiences, or at least some of them, to learn. You can't shortcut that for me. This is a model here of learning which presupposes that the teacher is going to be a facilitator – not a fount of wisdom, not a source of knowledge. For in experiential learning, we are concerned with much more than knowledge, we are concerned with the development of competence and capability, for which the teacher is therefore a facilitator.

Look at the diagram again. Imagine that it's on one side of a Toblerone packet; and then imagine that on the other side of the packet, the other sloping side, we have a similar loopy diagram which describes what the teacher does. If you can picture these loops of reflection, you will note that as you come up to the peak of the loops, soon there will be an intimate contact between the teacher and learner - contact in which the teacher is asking questions, the teacher is hearing responses, the teacher is looking at work, the teacher is sharing experience. But then the learner goes off into the next surge of activity, away down there on the bottom of the side of the Toblerone packet. The teacher hasn't departed; but the teacher is separated, there merely as someone to resource, someone to structure activities, but not someone intimately holding the learner's hand as you have your experience as a learner. The teacher is a facilitator, not an instructor.

The last point is that there are three types of reflection; and this is where that diagram is different from Kolb's. There is the reflection that looks forward and says 'Where do I want to go?': the reflection in the first loop. There is the reflection in the intermediate loop that is partly looking back and saying 'How did that exploratory experience go?' and immediately looking forward and saying 'What do I want to do next?' Then there is the appraising experience at the end which is very much a consequence of the teaching – judging what has been done against criteria. Appraising isn't *only* judging what has been done against criteria; it is formulating these criteria as well. So this is the appraisal that says 'Have I made enough progress to please me, and others perhaps, at the moment? Do I wish now to move on and to concentrate for a while on other items on my agenda?'

Comment

That, I believe, is what we currently know about the way adults learn through experiential learning. In the present context my summary reminds me of Molière's character Monsieur Jourdain, who was discussing what prose was. Eventually the idea dawned on him, and he said 'So, if I ask my maid Nicole to go and get my slippers for me because I'm going to bed; then I'm talking in prose?'. His teacher said 'Yes'. And Monsieur Jourdain exclaimed 'Mon Dieu, you know I've talking in prose for forty years and I never realised it'. In many of the schools of art and design with which I've been acquainted, most of the pedagogical principles I've described are enshrined already in best teaching practice. It may be that they are not done consciously; it may be that they are not done with the sort of a diagram I've used in mind, but there is a lot of good practice which very much exemplifies sound learning theory.

In my own university the most important staff development need to me is that of my most able tutors, and of my most able academic colleagues. For I believe that the good health of an institution is promoted by helping very good people to fulfil their potential to be excellent. So I suggest that the fact that you are doing something to a reasonable or a good standard is not a reason for failing to scrutinise practice, or to ask a few questions.

Questions to Ponder

These are the questions that I would ask if I was a part-time teacher in one of the art institutions, thinking about best practice in teaching, and trying to carry it further forward.

Firstly, do we give enough thought to the relationship between these two types of activity in the model, and the building up of a sequence that links them together? That's where I would expect some of the purposefulness of teaching to come. For my defini-tion of teaching is not derived from the instructional mode, but from facilitation where good teaching is 'the purposeful creation of situations from which learners shouldn't escape without learning or developing'. By 'the purposeful creation of situations' I mean that, as a teacher, I've got to have purpose and know what I'm aiming for – though not necessarily that the students will emerge with learning which I have planned in detail for them. I believe I need to think more and I do think more, in my discipline, about the purposeful linking of these two styles of activities in their developing sequence.

The second question I would ask myself is the one that I did ask at Wimbledon, 'How do we know what is good practice in teaching?' When, in my educational research, I took recorded protocols from teachers and from learners about how they engaged in creative activities, what the teachers *told* me they did in their own creativity often wasn't what they *actually* did. And how they told students to do it wasn't the same as either of these. And what students actually did was different again. It may not be so in your discipline, and that's fine if you know so and if you've enquired. *I* enquired, and the discrepancies I found worried me. So nowadays I always feel I need to think very hard about what is good practice. And how do I know what is effective practice? The answer to that ques-tion relates to what your definition of teaching is, and not what mine is.

The third question asks how to put more emphasis on the intermediate reflection, which is the reflection which has produced the biggest pay-off for me, in terms of the improvement of creativity of my students. There is a lovely picture that Gordon Pask has, of the creative learner who is struggling with a task, and is in a confusing maze. A schizophrenic part of that learner climbs out, and standing on a platform a little above it all, looks down and says 'You know, I see how I can do that and I see how I can do it a little better'. The reflective part is that which comes out of you and just for a little while is capable of observing constructively.

I'm not suggesting that we should engage in navel gazing all the time that we are doing anything. That would be crazy. For instance, if Jacky Stewart is driving around Hyde Park Corner in the rush hour, and somebody changes lanes and is about to bump into him, what he does is what would be called intuitive. But a capable driver like Jacky Stewart can tell you in much finer detail than the average person exactly what he is doing at that moment with his body and with his brain – if he chooses to be so aware. It is interesting that in research into the thought processes of the able people in many of the creative and problem-solving activities, what is found is the ability to be aware and the knowledge of how they do what they do. I certainly found a pay-off for my students in helping them to reflect on process in that way.

Finally, if you have a vision of the reflective part watching the active part of you, one of the limitations is that you usually only climb up on to one part of the observational platform. The role that any kind of facilitative interaction can play in reflection is to encourage the learner to go to a different part of the platform, and to look at their activ-ities and see them with a different perspective. That can be the most creative influence of all. I've actually been an Open University student for the past three years, because I thought that was a good way to keep in touch with what open learning is about. At times

I've been trying to analyse what kind of facilitative comments from others further my development as a learner I've found that the most useful facilitative comments to me are the ones that encourage me to move to another position on my reflective platform, from which I see myself from a different perspective. Facilitative tutors don't drag me to another position (I resist that); they encourage me, and lead me to see myself different- ly. I think that's why and where practitioners coming in from outside have a particular- ly relevant role to play in teaching, in Art and Design.

Evaluation

Does the model work? Well I've tried to build on reflection, at first year level, and I've tried to build on it at third year level. At first year level, the net result was that my stu- dents did a lot better in design competitions in Scotland (organised by an outside body) than they had done previously; and they did better than the students from other simi- lar departments. It may have been my enthusiasm and so on which led to the improve- ment; but it does seem that something made a difference. One of the differences that it made was that, if the students were observed by people who didn't know what they were observing, they noticed that Heriot-Watt's students behaved in a different way. They divided their time in a different way, during a creative problem-solving activity. At third year level (in a four year course), I've emphasised reflection and an awareness of process in the midst of what learners are doing. I found that the employers on the milkround seemed to feel that there was a change in the quality of the people that we were pre- senting to them for interview. That's why I believe in this business of reflective aware- ness as the key to progress – once you've adopted the model I described.

Reflection by Teachers

If we are encouraging learners to be aware of process, I would also apply that same demand to teaching, if it is to be validly seen as a profession. To me, one of the concepts associated with the word 'profession' is that it has a core of knowledge which is gener- ally accepted, which comes out of experience, and which has been tested – and as things stand at the moment is reasonably proven.

If we are engaged in education, we presumably think that there is a profession of edu- cation – the education of our discipline. I think that calls on us to go back to my model and sometimes to stop in the midst of what we are doing, and ask 'What are the process- es that lead to effective learning for our students?' Now, one of the great problems I find in my teaching is that it's difficult to find ways of discovering what happens for the stu- dent as a result of what I do as a teacher. It's as if I've put messages in bottles, even if it's during a dialogue. Do my bottles reach the other shore - the learner? And when they reach the other shore, if the bottle's uncorked, what kind of a condition are the messages in? What effect do they have? Some teachers are now engaging in very creative formu- lative evaluation techniques which lead to a much richer, deeper and more informed dialogue between students and teachers. It turns both into action researchers of the stu- dents and of the teachers' own personal development in their professional area, includ- ing the educational aspect of it.

Art education and the scrutineers

ANDREW BRIGHTON

Leader, School of Cultural and Supporting Studies,
Kent Institute of Art and Design

Art education is surely not alone in higher education in seeing the rise to power of a stratum of administrators with little academic distinction or professional reputation. It is a symptom of a wider change in the ordering of society, and its consequences for art education have broader implications.

When Michel Foucault wanted to describe the characteristics of the distinctly modern disciplining of society he chose as his central analogy the panoptic prison design by Jeremy Bentham. In Bentham's design the prison is a circular building like a barrel. The walls consist of cells which look into a rotunda, and at its centre stands a watchtower. Between each cell is a solid wall but the wall facing the watchtower is open. Each individual prisoner was to have a constant sense that he or she was under surveillance, whether or not surveillance was taking place. Modern discipline worked by training souls. Each of us has been trained to survey ourselves as if surveyed.

Scrutiny is changing. Post-modern humankind has no soul. We are not assumed to have some common essence, some shared moral core. Rather than self-discipline, now we have to be seen to perform. Public sector educational institutions have been required to make themselves, their departments and individuals working for them systematically monitorable. Having defined their roles, aims and objectives and reordered their activities towards maximum efficiency, they can now be monitored internally and externally against established goals. 'Performance indicators' and the like enable evaluation by people empowered by their managerial position rather than their knowledge of a particular subject.

Managerial rationality is becoming a master discourse claiming directive power over other discourses in ways reminiscent of Marxist-Leninism. All can be known and evaluated within its systematic conceptions. There is, for instance, something Lysenko-like about the calculation of 'value addition' in higher education. Judging institutions and the value of what they do by quantitative methods may do for education what Lysenko's attempt to enforce evolutionary adaptation upon the potato did for Soviet agriculture.

Starting in 1989 the Conference for Higher Education in Art and Design (CHEAD, an association of principals and heads of colleges and departments of art and design) and the Council for National Academic Awards (CNAA, was the national body that confered non-university degrees) organised a series of conferences and papers on art and design education. Reading these documents shows art education reshaping itself for the scrutineers with seeming indifference to its own academic character.

Art speaks in complex utterances and this makes it inherently anomalous to managerial rationalism. It speaks sensually and conceptually. It is a theoretical, intuitive and a material activity. Characteristically it relies on the repetition of manual acts while valuing the disruptive. It can be read as a knowing sign and unknowing symptom. It is meta-physical, it speaks of absences through its material presence. Semiologically its signs can be iconic, indexical, nonce and arbitrary at one and the same time.

For fine art education this complexity is fundamental. The acquisition of manual skills cannot be divorced from concepts. The way something is carved, painted, drawn, or the way a photograph is developed, or shots are selected for a video, signify meanings and assumptions. These skills are in part acquired by repetition and imitation. They are acquired as much by example as by discursive instruction. They are in part what Michael Polanyi in his book *Personal Knowledge* called tacit knowledge, which is com-municated by demonstration rather than in theoretical principle. These are, in other words, complex skills. The initial CNAA/CHEAD paper was entitled 'On Not Sitting with Nellie'. This silly title celebrated the consequence of the decline in the ratio of staff to students; the tradition's one-to-one tutorial has become almost impossible, i.e. no more 'sitting with Nellie'. Serious and lengthy tutorial examination of a student's work is to be joyously swept away as teachers become the monitors of students' fulfilment of course objectives. The 'Nellie' document is about de-skilling fine art education of those skills that are peculiar to it and turning staff into performance scrutineers. These obser-vations are not intended as abuse. I know, like and respect some of the authors of 'Nel-lie'. But the fact is that the sole source of recognition they have for their abilities is from the management of educational institutions and national bureaucracies that have given them posts and placed them on committees. They are not artists of standing. They do not have within the political economy of their own careers, education and experience the grounds for critical independence from educational management. This point I am sure is not lost on those who appoint them.

In the 'Nellie' document a group of these course managers without the backing of either high professional reputations or systematic research and theoretical argument set out the 'imperatives for change'. The vision presented is essentially about new forms of academic administration and scrutiny. For example, what sounds like the statement of a profound if familiar truth, 'students learn independently', refers to a mode of course organisation used and advocated by one of the working party. 'Art and design education *must* (my emphasis) accept that in future control of the individual student's programme will ultimately lie with the student.' The doubtful assumption here is that a student developing their own work within a single course has less control and independence than one obliged to negotiate through a range of units of study. There is no evidence offered that this 'pioneering work in art and design' improved the education of its stu-dents. Gone, it seems, are the days when an art school became a model of practice because the quality of the work of its students and graduates was outstanding.

The drift of the document is to present the cuts in the per-student expenditure as nothing but a gain with no losses. In the future students will relate to the administrative system rather than to a particular discipline. They will choose from a menu of pedagogic units. But this individualising means that each student will pass from one pedagogic moment of scrutiny to another rather than being part of a group of students developing through common academic concerns, work and discussion.

Fine art education has been an initiation into a community of discourse and visual practice. The level of a student's understanding was made evident and assessed by their work. Assessment was by standards appropriate to particular pieces of work and the general demands of the kind of practice the student had chosen to develop. In the logic of unitisation, modularisation and credit accumulation assessment criteria are supplied by the aims and objectives of the course unit not by the nature of student's own developing practice.

'Nellie' may be part of a movement to a relatively lower level 'mass' undergraduate education in this country modelled on the United States. To plan such moves without admitting loss of specialist quality at undergraduate level is dishonest and to do it without consideration of the educational context of British students is dangerous. Public sector education stands a good chance of combining the disadvantages of both systems and the advantages of neither by adopting one section of a more protracted system of education. Modularisation, unitisation and credit accumulation may make sense within a system which offers and values a much more broadly based education up to degree level. But in the US this is a part of a much longer period of post school education in which far more students go on to specialist postgraduate degrees.

At a national conference in Liverpool in October 1989 heads of art and design schools and departments were gathered together in the sight of the CHEAD and the CNAA. The academic guarantors, overseers and managers of art education had been sufficiently pleased with the Nellie document to use it as the basis for a series of regional and then this national conference. In the report of that event it appears that the people who are in day to day control of art and design courses found it unnecessary or were incapable of criticising the managerial logic they faced. They seemed unaware or indifferent to the way in which matters of academic management have consequence on what is taught and learnt. (It has been claimed by some participants that dissent was simply not recorded.)

Take one instance at the heart of art education: in the papers and conference reports there is no fundamental discussion of the differences between art and design. They are very different cultures shaped in part and perhaps invigorated by antipathy. After all, some fine art practice has claimed to stand critically, ironically or reflexively apart from mass communication and market value. The 'Nellie' document tells us that the broad educational objectives common to all art, design and craft programmes include 'the ability to relate to markets'. The political and resource benefits of lumping together of art and design seems to have silenced any academic objections to homogenisation.

This has direct implications for how students are taught and assessed. The authors of the 'Nellie' document write: 'We suggest that a common "resources bank" of skills, with different emphases according to the predicted outcomes of the course, can be identified as appropriate to all graduates and diplomats from higher education in art, design and craft.' The difference between skills used in both art and design is a difference of paradigm not merely of emphasis.

Amongst the listed common skills is 'Criteria for analysis and evaluation of own and other's work'. The assumption that there can be common criteria for art suggests the authors are innocent of the theory of their subject. For instance, in traditional Kantian aesthetics there can be no criteria for aesthetic judgements, judgements of art are conceptless, they are concerned with intuitive experience. Or we might take the view from the 'Institutional Theory of Art' that art is a contested concept. What characterises objects or acts treated as art is that they become the object of argument. In other words, works of art are not sites for the application of criteria rather they are sites for debates about criteria.

As reported, the Liverpool conference advocated making the criteria of judgements in student assessment explicit as if this was entirely unproblematic. The report even calls for 'tangible criteria'. In other words, the academic leadership of art and design intensified the misdescription of how judgements are made in art. The proceedings of subsequent conferences have yet to be published but from what I can glean they advance the progress of management rationality into art rather than resisting it.

With the combination of decreasing resources per student and the keener rules of scrutiny, serious undergraduate fine art education may have little or no future in public sector education and there is little of it in the universities. But I suspect the situation is not unique. The discourse of educational management and that of many academic disciplines are incommensurable. As the power of management grows students will increasingly undergo an educational process of jumping through hoops rather than an initiation into a discipline which has a reflective life independent of managerial rationality. In education kinds and levels of knowledge and practice are being devalued and may be extinguished.

One reason why the decline in art education may go unrecorded is because of its inarticulacy. We are poor at describing and theorising what we do. The discourse of art is particularly distant from the discourse of management and few people seem to be outstanding in both. Not enough of us are bilingual. This inarticulacy, this inadequate theoretical base is not just a problem in defending what we do. It is a problem in developing what we do and in doing what we do well. To make an obvious point that seems to go unnoticed, the predominant medium of art school teaching is words, it is a discursive practice. The value of the artist as teacher is presumably that they can communicate their grasp of the complexity of art utterances by discursive example. Tutoring people making art is tutoring people in ways of thinking about art.

But one of the things I most consistently find is an incapacity of art students to read their own work or the work of others. They are not equipped to think their way into the actuality of a work. We now have a situation where many recent graduates of any half-alive art history department have a more literate and imaginative understanding of past and contemporary practice than most art school graduates behind whose thin visual practice stands the common sense of the studios. The underdeveloped discursive culture of art in English art schools culturally disempowers students.

Why is this the case? One reason is the role we played in establishment culture. It seemed that all the art educator had to do when threatened by change was to get Patrick Heron to ask one of his old Etonian friends to write a protest letter to the *Guardian*. Such letters used to work because there has been in the liberal establishment a sentimental attitude to art education. Art education was to be the opposite of academic education. It was where people were 'expressive' and 'creative', it was a place for educational anomalies, for wonderfully gifted, virtually dumb, perennial adolescents. Serious art is not, in my view, a therapeutic activity nor a conceptless gush of pure visuality. It is a medium of ideas as well as sensuality and feeling. We were patronised into a kind of academic idiocy by our establishment liberal friends.

I think our notion of the artist is too anti-academic and too market influenced. This is not altogether our fault; the museums of modern art, such as the Tate, celebrate and reify the defeat of the academies and the rise of the free market over the last one hundred and fifty years. Academicism is a theorised conception of art. The market's defeat of the academies has become so habitual that we can not use 'academic' as an approbatory term to describe an artist/teacher who explores in their work explicitly a particular conception of art.

Another problem is that the market from which most art schools take their models of practice has been the New York dominated international art market. In this we are provincials. We are usually far removed from the ideas, values and critical debates that formed what is taken to be exemplary practice. This art tends to be understood as an appearance to be read within a long-established English art school common sense. This common sense stripped down to its essentials tends to go something like this: artists are especially chosen people. They are not simply people who make art, they are in themselves unique beings with a special way of seeing the world. Great art works are ideologically transcendent objects usually made by heroic men. The capacity to recognise great art is a speechless instinct amongst the chosen people of art. This view was in the past marshalled chronologically and cannonised by art history and it is certainly reinforced by most media arts coverage. Obviously for brevity's sake this is a gross caricature and even some of the apparently disparaged characteristics can be argued from another side. For example, the idea of the artist's heroic role to tell the truth has been an important one in Eastern and Middle Europe at least from Tolstoy to Vaclav Havel. Further, I am a committed pluralist, I am not here concerned with condemning a particular set of beliefs. My point is that inasmuch as art school studio common sense teaches a theory of no theory it is not self-aware; it takes its own assumptions as self-evident truths.

In my view its dominance serves students ill, stultifies academic development, makes art education an ideological chameleon incapable of understanding and defending itself.

The artist/teacher: Roles, models and interactions

CLIVE ASHWIN

Professor Emeritus, Middlesex University

The role of the artist as teacher is as old as art itself, but the character and context of that role have changed historically and continue to change, creating many variations in the forms of interaction between artist and art student.

It may be difficult to imagine life without the existence of institutions such as art schools, colleges and academies. But this was more or less universally the case before about 1500. Until the end of the fifteenth century, the training, education and preparation of artists was, as with so many skills and professions, entirely in the hands of practitioners. Typically, the aspiring artist in any medium would enlist in the workshop, *bottega* or *atelier* of a practising artist and undertake a lengthy period of training and preparation, beginning with the most menial tasks of grinding and mixing colours, preparing grounds, fetching and carrying, and acting as general dogsbody.

We have to imagine a world without mass-produced paint in tubes, a world in which travel and transport was slow and difficult, in which prints were a valuable rarity and books, for most, an inaccessible luxury. Physical proximity to the artist and the studio was the principal or only means of gaining access to the information, skills and know-how needed to become an artist. The head of a studio provided not only a model in terms of technical performance and artistic taste, but an example in terms of professional ethics, ranging from simple value-for-money to more exalted judgements of artistic worth.

> The artist is an educated man,
> skilled is he.
> Sensible, resourceful, clever and reticent;
> all these must a good artist be.
> A true artist works with glad heart,
> patiently and without haste,
> with care he goes about his work,
> creates it with skill,
> builds it up and devises its shape.
> He gives order to his matter,
> makes all into a whole, harmoniously.
> A bad artist,
> careless and sanctimonious is he,
> mocks men, deceives people.
> He is a thief!

These lines, dating from the fifteenth century, illustrate the intersection of art and morals. The poem was translated from a manuscript produced by an Aztec poet working in Mexico before the Spanish conquest, but it manifests a sentiment which is almost universal in societies, that one cannot reduce professional practice to a matter of technical performance alone. There is always a moral dimension, in terms ranging from the quality of execution to dedication to certain standards of loyalty to artistic vision. In all these, the practising artist provided a mentor and model for the aspirant and novice.

During the closing years of the fifteenth century the monopoly of art training held by artists themselves was breached by the foundation of the first academies of art, initially in some of the city-states and courts of Italy, and subsequently throughout Europe. At first there was a clear division of responsibility. The academies concentrated on the increasingly complex theoretical aspects of art practice, such as anatomy, perspective and architectural detail, while the studios continued to deal with the necessary craft skills involved in fabrication, such as the preparation and use of materials and grounds, modelling, casting and the practical management of contracts. This division of responsibilities was reflected in the fact that within the walls of the early academies the pupils drew, but did not paint, sculpt or model. These activities were regarded as the province of the studio, within which the student remained in constant contact with the practitioner.

As the years passed and centuries unfolded, the number of academies multiplied, and they were joined by a growing variety of institutions. To the national and royal academies, one must add the numerous private *ateliers* of nineteenth-century Paris, in which successful artists expanded their practice into a thriving education business. Then, increasingly in the nineteenth century, states and great cities launched and provided for schools of art and design; most of our existing colleges and faculties in the UK date from this great period of expansion. Often, institutions were transmogrified in the course of their history, as in the case of the former Hornsey School of Art, founded as a private art school in 1881 and later assimilated by a local education authority, and now a university faculty.

Over the course of four centuries of evolution, the functional relationship between the artist's studio and the institution as a training ground for artists changed. For complex social, cultural and economic reasons, the former went into decline and, with a few notable exceptions, the latter became entirely responsible for the education and training of artists. In this context, the role of the artist/educator changed to that of an employee of the institution. Nevertheless, this arrangement could work well. Our own artistic tradition has increasingly become dependent upon the role of the art school as a meeting point, a nexus of cultural transmission and development in which the art of the past and present stimulates and guides the art of the future.

It is often popularly assumed that the processes of organised educational provision play little or no part in the preparation and formation of artists, and that it is common for artists to achieve excellence and public notice with little or no reference to art schools and colleges. In the mid-1970s I examined this belief in detail, with reference to a sample of one hundred British artists of note working at that time. My principal conclusion was basically simple, that few artists achieve any kind of public acclaim and notice without attendance at one or more art schools, and often for prolonged periods of time. My research did not claim that their experience was particularly good or valuable, but it did dispel, for better or worse, the notion of the common 'natural' artist and the exclusive autodidact.

The forms of interaction between artist as teacher and artist as student are as numerous as artists themselves, but there are some common models which illustrate the varieties of that relationship. Who can imagine Sickert without his mentor Whistler? It was under Whistler's direction that Sickert acquired his sublime mastery of tone, the most important formal ingredient of his greatness as a painter. And it was in emulation of Whistler's artistic philosophy and personal style that Sickert learned to paint dangerously, to eschew the over-resolution of subject and to make the spectator work to resolve meanings. Whistler was not over-endowed with altruism, and no doubt one reason for inviting Sickert into his studio was that Sickert had something of value to give him, and this retroactive benefit is a feature of the artist/student relationship which we cannot ignore.

One does not have to be a great or significant artist to give something of value to those destined for higher things. Few would now recognise the name of Lecoq de Boisbaudran, but the names of some of his students, which include Rodin, Fantin Latour, Legros and Dalou, represent an important sector of late nineteenth-century art.

The transaction between teacher and student is rarely one of simple transmission or formation. Just as important is what psychologists call 'reaction-formation', in which the process of kicking against authority is a crucial element of self-realisation. The young Pre-Raphaelites abhorred the easy rhetoric of the Royal Academy school, still in their day under the thrall of 'Sir Sloshua Reynolds'. They rejected the grandiloquent stock gestures and gloomy suggestive areas of canvas. Like over-zealous members of a neighbourhood watch scheme, they moved into the picture, improved the ambient lighting to reveal what was going on in the corners, listed accessories in detail, and examined personal motives scrupulously. Perhaps the same process of reaction-formation played a part in the development of Gilbert and George, who attended St Martin's School of Art during the 1960s when it was most characterised by the monumental physicality of Caro and his followers. Their response was to deny the customary physical substance of the sculptural object by substituting documentation, and ultimately by dissolving it into the flux of life itself. These and many other kinds of relationship between artist as teacher and artist as student have continued to recur throughout history, whether in the context of the private studio or the public institution.

The historical development that I have rapidly sketched is not intended to eulogise or celebrate the history of art education, nor the role of artists within that history. But we must at least recognise that our artistic tradition, with all its virtues and defects, has rested very heavily on the interaction of artists of different generations within the context of the institution. In the past twenty years we have seen a profound transformation of the nature of that relationship, largely as a result of economic pressures.

The 1960s was a decade of optimism and expansion in higher education, including art education. Teaching posts, part-time and full-time were not too difficult to find for the capable, qualified and energetic. Indeed, it was not unknown for them to be secured by the incapable, unqualified and indolent, although, of course, we hope that these were in an insignificant minority. Practising artists and designers often undertook one or two days teaching a week at an art school, providing students with a valuable interface with the realities of practice, and at the same time benefiting from their different points of view, not to mention the money. I believe that much of the best of our artistic tradition up to the 1960s and 1970s, benefited from this process of symbiosis between artists, students and institutions.

In the late 1970s this situation was overtaken by major economic pressures. The mood of optimism and expansion of the 1960s was replaced in the 1970s by a growing awareness of the true cost of the scale of higher education provision which we had created post-war. For the first time local authorities and colleges became seriously concerned that they had reached the bottom of the public purse, there was no more money, and they could not make ends meet. The largest component of the budget of most educational institutions is the salary costs of full-time staff. One way of minimising expenditure was to disguise full-time vacancies as several part-time posts, reducing both costs and contractual liabilities. Staff who would formerly have sought and probably gained a full-time post in one institution, secured two days at one college, two days at another, and maybe an afternoon at a third. In large institutions, the internal accounting system might not have been sufficiently tight to detect that the same lecturer was accumulating pieces of teaching on different courses or in different faculties without anyone grasping the scale of the institution's involvement as an employer.

In 1978/9 the dam burst. As a result of a now famous legal case which granted recognition of continuity of employment to a lecturer on a part-time contract, large numbers of staff on part-time contracts successfully applied for recognition as permanent employees of institutions. In some cases they were already working hours in excess of the maximum recognised for full-time staff. Many of the part-time staff who acquired permanant status in the 1979 debacle, either as full-time employees or as permanent fractional appointments, were and remain valuable lecturers and managers. In some ways, their route for joining the tenured staff was more rigorous and selective than completing an application form and impressing an interview panel one fine day in April.

However, in some cases the only qualification for tenure achieved in this way was the fact that the applicant knew and worked well with one key member of the staff, sometimes a course leader, but in some cases another lecturer or an old college friend. I don't think that anyone can honestly defend such an arbitrary way of staffing our colleges on a regular basis.

The upheavals of 1979 had a whole series of consequences which proved detrimental for art colleges and their students. Panicked by the growing insecurity of employment, most part-time staff sought tenured posts unless they had a very strong reason for not doing so. The old game of part-timers' musical chairs, in which staff moved relatively freely between colleges, came to an abrupt halt when the music of financial liquidity ceased. If you were lucky enough to be sitting on a chair when the music stopped, you seized the seat with both hands until your knuckles went white.

The effects upon the management of institutions were equally deleterious. In order to head-off possible future claims for continuity of employment, management imposed restrictions upon the size of contracts of remaining part-timers which made life difficult for everyone. The unions played, I regret to say, a dubious role, on the one hand expressing scorn and outrage at the limitation of contracts, on the other supporting all arguable cases for tenure.

As the funding crisis deepened, management cast about for some financial sacrificial lamb to make the books balance. Most components of a institutional budget, such as full-time salary costs, cannot be reduced or varied, and certainly not on a short timescale. The only budget head of any size which was susceptible to quick reduction was the part-time hours budget, and this head was repeatedly raided to cover deficits elsewhere. A *post hoc* rationale was devised to justify this process, chiefly by reducing the part-time hours equivalent of a full-time vacancy.

Managers at the sharp end of provision, such as course leaders and deans, saw the writing on the wall. Part-time hours were clearly the soft underbelly of resource provision, repeatedly raided and sliced away, layer by layer. Their natural reaction was to escape from this threat as quickly as they could, if possible by firming up part-time staff into fractional posts, or by cumulating them into full-time appointments.

There were numerous harmful secondary consequences of this process. A rich retinue of part-time staff is of immense value when it can be reorganised from term to term to suit changing curricular needs. It is not so useful when it becomes set in concrete as a bizarre mosaic of bits and pieces; when it is difficult or impossible to modify hours of contact and shift them about within the week in response to new requirements. Even more acutely, institutions may find themselves stuck with lecturers who might have been employed to provide a valuable, topical and timely input at one historical moment. As time passes, what they have to offer may become increasingly marginal and irrelevant.

I don't have any immediate solutions to this problem but I would recommend the following steps to protect and foster the invaluable role of part-time teachers.

1. Institutions should formulate and try to maintain a balanced proportion of full-time, fractional, and part-time staff.
2. There should be a long-term national agreement and guidelines on the contractual situation, in particular to prevent further part-time staff from gaining tenure by accident.
3. Institutions must ensure that their management and information systems are sufficiently tight to prevent evasion of contractual ceilings and the making of permanent appointments by stealth.

Although the situation looks fairly gloomy at the moment, we should be cheered by the thought that in the course of time staff will resign, retire, or leave for other reasons. In the process of reconstructing staff complements, institutions should bear clearly in mind and protect that uniquely valuable contribution to be made by the genuine part-timer, who spends the other part – often the majority – of his or her week in meaningful professional practice.

'Campus Camp'

Jon Thompson

*Head of Fine Art, Goldsmiths' College,
University of London*

I want to preface my paper with one very simple statement, and that is that I am, have been, and remain always a firm supporter of the idea of artist-teachers in art schools. Historically at Goldsmiths' College we have maintained the lowest possible number of full-time members of staff and the highest possible number of part-time members of staff, who are all practitioners in theory or in practice in the remainder of their time.

But I don't think that the notion of the artist-teacher is quite as simple and as easy to justify as we have been led to believe; it has problems on many levels. Speaking as a practitioner and an artist who exhibits, I have enormous difficulty sustaining both my practice and my teaching at the optimum level, and I expect that this is true of most people in that position. It is a form of state patronage in many ways. It's probably the largest form of state patronage in the arts, and yet it could be argued that it does as much damage to the artist as it does to the education system. So I am not quite so sanguine about the argument that it is automatically the case that artists teach art better than anybody else. I think it is essential that artists teach art, but there are other ingredients as well.

I want to trade Harry Thubron's quotations with Andrew Brighton's. Harry was the first person who ever indicated to me (and it was in my first years of teaching at an art school) that there was any problem in art schools. I had drifted through St Martin's and the Royal Academy Schools; we'd all been jolly friends together and I'd never learned to think very much really, and what I had learnt I felt to be highly problematic only four or five years later. I should add that both schools were full of practising artists; it's not as though they were devoid of practitioners. At St Martin's alone, I think we had about ten Academicians teaching us how to portrait paint – the relevance was never questioned. It was just taken to be automatic – they were practising artists, they knew, they transferred their skills to me and off I went. And what did I do with those skills? I became a society portrait painter.

It was not true that somehow the Coldstream report ushered in a phase where for the first time practising artists entered into British art schools – the teachers were all practising artists in one way or another. When I first taught at Lancaster, a printmaker there was selling prints faster certainly than I've ever sold any art in my life. He was a full-time professional printmaker, a practising artist. He had nothing to offer to the students, but that was never questioned. In fact he got them off the presses fast so that he could get his own editions on! The notion that the Coldstream report was responsible for some kind of rosy glow in the art education world that we all look back on nostalgically ever since is not true.

When I came back from Rome my first job was in Lancaster College of Art, and I met Harry Thubron again. In the bar one night he commented: 'Jon, the enemies of art are in the art schools. And mostly they are running them.' And that was the first time any-body had ever indicated to me that there was any problem. But it has come back to haunt me as a quotation ever since. I think that it has almost always been true, that the ene-mies of art are in the art schools, and mostly they have been running them, and they will go on running them I suspect.

Something else very interesting that he said was directly about artist-teachers: 'One of the problems with artists teaching is that so many of them see their role as that of cast-ing artificial pearls before genuine swine.' I think, thank God, that it is a lot less true today that the role of the artist-teacher was an occasion for often quite dreadful abuse of the learning situation. And I think, strangely enough, that improvement followed the introduction of foundation courses, where the whole question of how one taught was dealt with as an experimental question in this country, probably for the first time. That began to breed a different attitude to the whole question of teaching, and set a different kind of standard for the artist-teacher.

Another memorable quotation comes from William Coldstream. It was in the Fitzroy Tavern, three days after Coldstream and the whole of the Coldstream Committee had resigned. He said to me (he was quite well-oiled – I think that was his term – it's a good term for a painter anyway, 'well-oiled'): 'You know, Jon, the problem is that we just do not have enough artists who are also good teachers to run the system.' And that was a man who had just resigned and a whole committee with him, after setting up the sys-tem, organising it, selecting the schools that were going to be approved, etc., over a sub-stantial period of time. And in many ways it was said in the tone of a kind of confessional. The system is fine, but we don't have the kind of manpower that would be needed ideally to run it.

That is something we may now need to look back on, because I think in many ways the system of English art education has always been too expanded, too overproductive and so on. In a paper I produced several years ago I pointed out that to justify the rough-ly 3,500 fine art graduates per year (a) argued that you had absolutely remarkable teach-ing resources and (b) that you had somewhere to put all these people. There are studio complexes up and down the country where the residue of various art schools – those people we have no place to fit, who have lost touch with their desire to be artists, etc., sit out their time painting objects which are on the whole incomprehensible. The question of the production of arts graduates, fine artists, and fine arts practitioners in this coun-try is not one we can simply ignore. It is a crucial question, which is the way the gov-ernment would like to see it. It is a question of how effectively you can do your job and what sort of people you have, what sort of resource you have to do it with.

Another quotation in a bar, this time in Milan, sets a slightly different parameter. It was at the opening of the *British Art Exhibition* in Milan in 1978 or 1979 – I can't remember which. We were sitting with Mario Mertz and one or two people. I said to Mertz: 'What do you think of British art?' And he said: 'Well, it's very well made.' I queried: 'You don't want to say any more than that?' 'No, that's it. It's very well made.' But it was said in a deeply critical tone of voice. It started me speculating as to precise-ly what he meant, and with one or two British artists who were representatives in the exhibition we talked about it. What we all thought he meant, and I think it was indeed what he did mean, was that in some way the objects of British art are largely over-determined. They are the product, in many cases, of extremely effective teaching that over-determines them in some way. They are well-made conceptually, well-made physically – all of those things, but they don't feel like art.

We could say that yes, we have one hundred and fifty years of the most effective, the most famous, the most expansive art education in the Western world, but it is often a good thing to pause from time to time and look at the effect of this.

The time is the early sixties, and the setting a wine bar off the King's Road. The now well-known West Coast American artist, Ed Ruscha, as he used to be called (I think he's now simply called Ruscha) was staying in London, and paying the occasional visit to Chelsea College of Art. I, too, was a visitor at Chelsea at the time. One day we had lunch together. I asked him what he thought of art schools, and his reply was a memorable one. 'They are the same everywhere,' he said. 'Full of teachers, camping it up pretending to be artists, and a lot of artists pretending to be concerned individuals. If it's not rape, then it is seduction.' Black and bleak and even cynical though this remark was – and it's typical of the man, he's a very dry character – I have cherished Ruscha's remark ever since, for two reasons. Firstly, I have always used it as a kind of negative touchstone against which to measure my own behaviour as a teacher. It is quite a salutary thing to ask yourself from time to time whose particular interests you have in mind. Are you genuinely helping them with their creative problems or are you forwarding your own philosophy of art at their expense, or even dominating or seducing them? And secondly, there is something in Ruscha's equation of pretence which has always seemed to me to perfectly encapsulate my dilemma as an artist-teacher.

The dilemma of the artist-teacher seems to me to be the difficulty of, on the one hand, fulfilling my duties as an effective role model, an exemplary figure who can show the way, even provide access to a greatly desired professional coterie and the lifestyle that goes with it, whilst at the same time providing knowledge of critical method, a great deal of hard information relating to theory, history and practice, as well as a wide range of insights covering everything from politics and culture through to more personally psychological, social and spiritual matters.

As an artist-teacher I am thus required to combine the necessary self-centred and self-seeking partiality of the artist with the careful solicitude and studious impartiality of a scholar priest. And if, in the process of achieving this extraordinary feat, I am at the same time to avoid committing rape or seduction, to use Ruscha's terms, I must achieve this miracle of integration whilst at the same time maintaining a high degree of objectivity, and measured neutrality where matters of belief are concerned, and a continuous awareness of the sensibilities, susceptibilities and vulnerabilities of each and every young artist in my charge.

Any reasonably intelligent, pedagogically concerned, but otherwise uninvolved outsider might be forgiven for dismissing such an educational role and such a task as being downright impossible. And so it would be if it were not for one very exceptional, important factor: the part that desire plays in the game of art and life, and in particular the part that desire plays in this game of chance encounters, intuition, and unsystematic knowledge that we call art education.

In my view it is this, this curious, unmeasurable, but forceful thing called desire which is the single most important factor in any thorough-going educational process, regardless of the subject to be addressed. It is desire which provides the site about which the teaching and learning transaction will find its most effective form. This is particularly true when the subject and object of desire is art. It must be that the shared desire for art is the pivotal point around which the delicate negotiations between artist and teacher, teacher and young artist, young artist and artist, occur. And it is here that partiality and impartiality are rendered indistinguishable, that oppression and deceptive persuasion hold little or no sway.

It was Ortega y Gasset who asked the rhetorical question: 'Who knows where the desire for art comes from?' He goes on: 'We know without a shadow of doubt when it is absent, and when it is there it is plain for all to see. But who knows where this desire comes from?' As Ortega knew full well, his question is without an answer. Nevertheless, it is a question that must be repeatedly asked, since it serves to remind us of art's proper place in that dark void that comes before reason. I need only look to myself to know the force of Ortega's question and to experience again the central mystery to which it points. For instance, I cannot remember a time when I did not draw, paint, shape things and build objects. I cannot remember a time, in other words, when I did not desire to make art, to be with art, to be an artist. This is true in the way I remember my life – looking back, the way in which my life always seems to have been cast. No doubt the social scientist would have great difficulty with such a romantic and unscientific proposition, and would argue for a more objective and more analytical approach to the question of my creativity. Desire, the social scientist would argue, must have its point of origin within an examinable constellation of social circumstances and social relationships. We need only search diligently into one's past, sift away the evidence and we inevitably reach a point of kindling, a point of generation which gave birth to one's desire for art. A person, a group of people, a place, a peculiarity of circumstances, no matter what. But of one thing we can be certain, it would be firmly set in this concrete world of social and material exchange.

But as an artist and as a teacher, I do not and cannot accept these arguments – the arguments of the social scientist. And this after six years of psychoanalysis during which time this ground was gone over and over *ad nauseam*. As arguments they simply do not square with my own experience. There is nothing in my background, in my family history which can explain this all-consuming but utterly irrational passion which guarantees me nothing – not peace of mind, not a living, not a roof over my head – and yet still persists. No, for me Ortega's question, though it allows no room for answer, nevertheless embodies an undeniable truth. No one knows and no one can know from whence the desire for art springs. And his qualifying statement in my experience seems to me to be true also.

As an artist and a teacher I know without a shadow of doubt when the desire for art is present in those young aspirant artists that I teach. And, at the risk of sounding arrogant, I know from their responses that they recognise with unerring certitude that it is present in me at least for some of the time. In other words, they know exactly when I have lost touch with my desire, when (to use Ruscha's term again) 'I am camping it up', either pretending to be an artist or pretending the role of professionally concerned ped-agogue – they know, in short, when my heart is in the right place and when it is not.

I would like to take this question of desire even further, and to examine its institu-tional implications. It is one thing to recognise the centrality of desire in the making of an artist and quite another to recognise and respect its implications for the planning of an educational programme. It is one thing to pay lip service to the notion that the most important and most precious characteristic that young artists need to have is a burning, irrational, some would say irresponsible, desire to do something and to be something, and another to design an educational operation which respects that desire absolutely and unconditionally, even fearlessly. Nevertheless, it seems to me that the consequences of accepting Ortega's model of creativity are clear, certainly insofar as they seem to point to an unavoidable principle, a principle which I have worked with in twenty years of leading the teaching of fine art at Goldsmiths' College. Namely, that in any education-al endeavour focused on the practice of art, desire for art and by implication the artist must be placed at the centre. And it is this principle that has most come under attack in recent years for very dubious institutional and political reasons.

I want to say more about this principle of making the artist central to the education-al process, because it is often misrepresented and misunderstood. Ultimately, the ques-tion is one of authority, and from where authority is derived. As an institutional animal – a paid hand, if you like – I juggle around with several different kinds of authority. That which is vested in me, by dint of my status within the institution, that which is lent to me by my academic reputation within the university, within what the university calls my 'subject', and that which I can invoke by recourse to some superior knowledge of histo-ry and tradition of practice. There are others, but it is not necessary to list them here. I would argue, and it is an important qualification to my central educational principle, that all of these versions of authority avail me nothing when the question of the quality of my desire for art is at stake. At this point, there can be no distinction between teacher and student, at least no authoritative one. And at this point it is a measuring of and a testing of mutually held desire for the unattainable. At this point it is a discourse between equals, between, in other words, artists who are together seeking after some-thing in hope and good faith and good trust.

To put the artist at the centre of the art education programme is to place a particular subject and a particular type and quality of discourse at its centre. This discourse is characterised by rigorous doubt which must, in the face of all forms of authority, be directed, pointed, shaped, not just by the student, the young artist, but also by the teacher. Certainly it permits no easy programmatisation of the learning process. And that is a hardship which I am afraid as teachers we all just have to live with.

Translations: The language of public accountability

Judith Chaney

Registrar for Art, Design and Performing Arts,
Council for National Academic Awards

My brief was somewhat different from that of the other contributors. It was to listen to the papers and to comment from the viewpoint of the body responsible for validating degree courses in fine art in colleges and polytechnics. I had expected to hear discussion of the role of practitioners in teaching and an attempt to analyse the distinctiveness of their contribution. I wondered whether the claims made about their role would fit with CNAA's approach to quality assurance. Since the language of art is not that of an organisation like the CNAA, I thought that it would be interesting see whether any differences were rooted in fundamentally different premises about higher education or whether they were a matter of semantics.

In fact, the conference has not focused on these matters and I shall therefore attempt to pick up some of the points made and put them in the general context of public accountability. I choose this as a focus because the most heartfelt comments at this conference have been directed at national policies which are felt to impinge on fine art in a particularly destructive way.

It is felt that there has been an attack on the artist-teacher, both full-time and part-time, through reduced levels of funding, through an overly managerial approach to college administration and too much monitoring and review done in too bureaucratic a manner which takes teachers out of the studio and into the committee room. To add insult to injury, all of this decline is being presented as progress in initiatives promoting changes in teaching and learning methods.

These are familiar points in which there is much truth. In placing them in the context of public accountability, I have two starting points. First, higher education in fine art in the Polytechnic and Colleges Funding Council (PCFC) sector is a wholly publicly funded activity and, as such, cannot be immune from the accountability which applies to all other subjects. Secondly, the higher education system itself is moving from an elite system encompassing some 14 per cent of the 18–21 group towards a mass system serving a wider age range and a greater proportion of the total population. Again, fine art will not be immune from the implications of this shift for funding, for the types of courses provided and for the modes of attendance. These two points are closely linked and form the sub-text of these proceedings.

There are many dimensions to accountability but two aspects, accountability for funding and accountability for quality, are relevant here. At the highest level of management of funding, the PCFC enters into a public expenditure compact with the Treasury; it has to convince the government of the day that the funding it bids for will be spent in line with the objectives set for higher education. Currently these are threefold: to expand student numbers, to maintain the quality of provision and to improve cost effectiveness. Put bluntly, we are asked to do more for less and keep the quality high. This is government policy and in my view, given the scale of the problem in other areas of education, in health and in the social services, it is likely to remain government policy whichever party is in power.

Jon Thompson asked whether we are producing too many fine art graduates, arguing that an acceptable level of resources might be achieved if funds were spread less thinly. Given the commitment to the expansion of numbers and to increasing access for social groups currently under-represented in the student population, it is most unlikely that this option would ever be available as a national policy. If it were to be an option, no one should be under any illusions as to what it would mean. It would involve lining up with the courses for vets and doctors as specialist, vocational courses and becoming subject to a strict control of entry numbers related to the employment demand in the labour market. I cannot think that such an option would provide a framework supportive of the diversity of fine art degrees or of anything like the current number of courses. Most of us are familiar with the patterns in the graduate destination statistics which show that fine art graduates have great difficulty in entering employment directly related to their courses of study and even three years after graduation, have high levels of unemployment when compared with other graduates.

The second aspect of accountability lies with institutions and courses and that is the responsibility for quality. In the PCFC sector this has been exercised through the CNAA system which for all its faults (and although I have flinched during the conference as the knife went in, I accept that there is substance in some of the points made) – for all its faults, it has the great virtue that it does not prescribe anything beyond the general requirements for any degree level course of study. Courses are considered in their own terms and it is up to course teams to determine what kind of course they wish to provide in the context of their own institutions.

You can see where these remarks are leading me. I believe that during the conference there has been a tendency to displace onto CNAA and other bureaucratic scapegoats problems which lie firmly within the ambit of course teams and colleges. Fine art is being asked to do no more and no less than any other subject when it is asked to be explicit about course objectives and the way in which resources are being used to achieve these objectives. Surely there is nothing inherently alienating about this approach either to the artist as a teacher or the teacher as an artist. The problem lies in the tension between the conception of fine art courses as vocational when funding levels are moving inexorably towards the levels associated with courses which are less specialised.

Most of the speakers have assumed that the role of fine art degree courses is to produce practising artists and that there is a consensus about what constitutes 'practice'. I am not sure that an easy consensus exists.

Glynn Williams argued that when the first degrees were set up it was accepted that practitioners would have a high profile as teachers, validation panel members, external examiners and would have an involvement in funding decisions. The quality of courses was linked to the quality of the artists who were involved with the courses. He was generous enough to admit that his presentation had a rosy tint, and indeed it had. A reading of CNAA's files would highlight a number of other features of the time which would balance the picture somewhat and emphasise the lack of consensus. They include a high incidence of complaints from colleges about decisions which appeared to be unduly influenced by personal rather than academic issues; the number of appeals by students about the conduct of assessments (higher than in any other subject covered by CNAA) which nearly always focused on the student's confusion about the criteria against which their work was being judged and complaints from students about casual attitudes to teaching. Not every teacher who did not turn up for his studio session was giving charismatic seminars in the pub.

Notwithstanding the commitment of many artists and the worth of their contribution, the balance between artists and teachers gradually changed. CNAA and fine art staff in colleges increasingly sought the opinion of their peers running other courses who understood the constraints and the opportunities that they, themselves, had to contend with. In this they mirrored a pattern in other subject areas where, in the early days of CNAA, validation panels were dominated by members from universities. As the system matured, polytechnic and college members began to predominate. The analogy is not exact but it is relevant.

I actually agree with Glynn in that I think the involvement of practising artists in validation is now too low although their involvement in external examining remains strong. In the forthcoming review of membership CNAA is planning to increase the number of professional artists on the Register of Specialist Advisers and to extend the range of professions associated with fine art represented amongst CNAA's specialist advisers.

I think the issue is not just the level of participation but having a clear idea of what artists have to contribute to a course and indeed, what is a practitioner? Jon Thompson spoke disparagingly of 'provincial warehouses full of fine art graduates.' Do these people count as artists? Presumably not in his terms, but then there are many different types of practice and the operation of the market plays a large part in the recognition accorded to them. The important question for colleges is how they choose to use the experience of different practitioners to best effect in their own courses. In other words, how contributions of artist-teachers can be linked into the looped pattern of learning that John Cowan described and into quality assurance systems.

I found Andrew Brighton's paper difficult because he starts from premises with which I agree but develops them towards conclusions which I disagree with and, indeed, find bizarre. Can he be serious in suggesting that it is probably not possible to run a true fine art course in the public sector? He drew our attention to the increase in the level of external scrutiny to which colleges are subject and to the intensification of managerial activity associated with them. He is right to link the two and I agree with him that the PCFC sector is overburdened in this respect. PCFC itself, HMI, CNAA and BTEC – who could disagree? I hope that the current DES deliberations about the future of higher education and quality assurance on both sides of the binary line will lead to a less burdensome but equally rigorous system.

In the meantime, I do not think that fine art has a heavier burden than any other subject or that it is impossible for fine art to set out the principles on which courses are designed and the criteria against which a course team would wish the quality of a course to be judged. I do not accept that fine art education is so opaque a process that it cannot be described in these terms. There is, of course, an element of mystery in all education; that is what makes it exciting. No one can predict the particular responses of individuals, the point at which things suddenly come together and the student surges forward, or the forms that creative work resulting will take. These things cannot be predicted and no one is asking fine art teachers to do it. But students do have a right to know what the programme of study they are signing on for entails; what will be taught, how it will be taught and what assumptions will be made about what students will do for themselves.

Making aims and objectives and thereby the criteria for assessment explicit does not mean that the distinctive criteria used in fine art will somehow be reduced or that the role of judgement in either assessment or course evaluation will be diminished. CNAA maintains the difference between validation and review, which has as its purpose ensuring that the threshold quality of the course as a degree level programme of study is maintained and the role of the examination system in judging the levels of quality of achievement of individual students. It is not the role of CNAA to rank courses according to the quality of their output.

I make no apologies for the fact that CNAA does not operate at the level of theory, it is not the role of a validating body to theorise the practice of a subject. I return to the strength of the CNAA system of peer review which is that it accepts the approaches of course teams and considers them in their own terms.

This is the spirit in which the two conferences on teaching and learning in art and design have been held. Of course, you cannot separate how something is taught from the question of what is taught, but in times of scarce resources we can urge staff to reflect on the way courses are run, to determine for themselves what the most important aspects of their course are and to experiment with changes which will help to sustain the distinctiveness of their course. Wimbledon's answer will be different from that of other courses and they from each other. The 'On not Sitting with Nellie' paper was meant to be provocative; it may have struck some wrong notes, it may have confronted people with things they would prefer to ignore, but the debate is much needed. In fact, the two teaching and learning conferences have had a good responses and some of the most interesting contributions were from fine art teachers.

Both Glynn and Andrew mentioned the volume of paper engulfing courses and I join them in their despair. Ultimately, the documentation for validation and monitoring is the responsibility of colleges, nonetheless my personal view is that CNAA's lack of prescription in this has served the system ill. If CNAA had issued pro-forma or even examples of brief submissions we could have avoided a lot of problems. Few seem to believe CNAA officers when they say that information should be presented in minimalist form. I can't emphasise enough that the familiar axioms of 'quality not quantity', and 'less is more' should be to the fore when documents are produced and internal monitoring systems are set up. Fortunately, some colleges have now got this well in hand.

Clive Ashwin's clear account of the history of the employment of part-time teachers in art schools emphasised the lack of movement of teaching staff and the staleness that can set in without the injection of new blood. This is a familiar picture to CNAA and one of the reasons that the Committee for Art and Design supports moves in colleges who do question their own practices in a reflective and constructive way.

Finally, I was moved by Jon Thompson's reference to the desire to make art as a drive which has a force beyond the rational will. I think that this drive for exploration, this desire to learn, characterises all who are immersed in their subject; the theoretical physicist and the literature specialist are at one with the artist in this. But it is one thing to pay lip service to the desire and another to design a course which respects that desire, challenges it and ensures that the integrity of the subject and the integrity of the award to which the course leads is maintained. This is the context within which we should be discussing the contribution of the artist as a teacher. This is the task that lies squarely with fine art teachers themselves.

Values in Art: Bases for
Making Judgements of Artistic Value

Chairman's Introduction to the Second Conference

CHRISTOPHER FRAYLING

Professor of Cultural History, The Royal College of Art

The theme of this conference, 'Values in Art: Bases for Making Judgements of Artistic Value' is very timely. I keep being sent policy documents about higher education in fine art which tell me why, in the terms of the policymakers, they consider fine art to be important, and they are not terms that everyone here can share. The arguments tend to be very strange, because they always go round the edge of fine art practice. 'Fine art stimulates design', we are told, or 'what artists do in the evening, designers do the following morning.' The classic example, certainly in the Royal College, being David Hockney's paintings in the semi-Egyptian style, from which Zandra Rhodes' textile collection a year or two later was indirectly derived. Secondly, 'fine art has had a great effect on the new media' we are told in policy documents – rock videos, and things like that – or even advertising. 'Fine art contributes centrally to the art economy', I read in a policy document recently. This argument would have no problem at all with this conference's theme. 'Where do you find values in art?' Well, you find them in the Sotheby's catalogue. Strange, that the same work should mean such different things in different contexts – a different use of 'value'. Another argument: you can teach all sorts of things 'through' fine art – to hijack once again Herbert Read's famous distinction between teaching to art and through art – you can do all sorts of things through fine art. You can teach manual skills, or visual skills, or perceptual skills and that is often used in policy documents as an argument, why we educate fine artists when a lot of them won't actually become professionals in that area. But again, it's all about craft skills, and the argument moves round the edges of what is I think intrinsic to fine art practice. So, a lot of pragmatic debates are going on at the moment, and being used for all sorts of different purposes, and I think it's very brave of the conference organisers to say: 'Look, I'm not interested in all those pragmatics today, I'm interested in a much more central question, which is to do with issues that are intrinsic to the art, not extrinsic (because the argument has been extrinsic for at least twenty years, I believe, amongst policy makers) and to talk about the values which may be embodied in fine art in and of themselves'.

There's a story in Royal College folk-lore, which I hope is apocryphal, about a professor (not of fine art, I hasten to add) who, when asked what was his line on ethics, replied that since he had only been living there for six months it was a little too early to say. ('Essex Prof.' jokes are the new thing.) It was not always thus. If we were discussing this question in the mid-eighteenth century or the late eighteenth century, when the Royal Academy Schools were founded, we would have absolutely no problem at all confronting head-on a debate about values in art. The debate would have been centrally about ethics and values and the human dimension – at least to judge by its published trace. Rousseau, on whether the arts were really civilising or not; Burke, on where beauty resides; Joshua Reynolds, replying to people who said that he should have 'mercantile considerations' when setting up the Academy: 'No,' he said in the First Discourse, 'if the higher arts flourish, the other considerations will follow of course' – and we have been arguing about that casual 'of course' for the last two hundred years. Or in the later nineteenth century, equally, the debate about art education would have been centrally about values and ethics. Ruskin and Morris, arguing that ethics should be reintroduced into aesthetics, the two having been separated. Thus Ruskin, on the South Kensington system: 'the most interesting art', he said, 'is that which proceeds from the heart, that which involves all the emotions, associates these with the head, yet as inferior to the heart, and the hand yet as inferior to the heart and head, and thus brings out the whole person'. And without any self-consciousness, documents about art education in the later nineteenth century could say things like that. Today, everyone would blush and run shrieking from the room because no one had mentioned unit costs in the same breath. And Henry Cole, the senior civil servant who masterminded our art education system, for better or worse (he also put the whole of Britain's railways on a single gauge, and some would argue that he did the same for art education): when he went home at night, in his diary (which is kept in the V&A), or in his journal of art and design (which was the first printed, regular journal of art and design ever), would start arguing intrinsic values; he might spend his daylight hours on committees, but he had no problem at all about discussing the fact that fine art practice was, as he suggested, autobiographical. The system, he says, is full of pragmatics, but the judgement of art and design should never be, because it is autobiographical – it's about people. And a senior civil servant, who decided on the structures and funding of art education, could say that without a trace of self-consciousness in the 1850s and 1860s.

But in the late twentieth century, I believe that much of that richness has gone in a welter of pragmatism, unit costs per student, degree statuses (what is a 'degree painting'?) and institutional arrangements. And the whole debate seems to have reduced itself to a kind of time and motion study of the circumstances surrounding fine art activity. So I believe very strongly that this discussion on 'Values in Art', which I take to be an attempt to redress the balance, is a brave thing to attempt: it is very much against the current of the sort of arguments that are intended to persuade people about the validity and importance of fine art activity today; and most educators – preferring to lead a quiet life – are swimming with the current, not against it.

What is aesthetic value?

ANTHONY O'HEAR

Professor of Philosophy, Bradford University;
art critic and writer

It is hard, and at first sight, not very rewarding, to analyse the nature of the aesthetic judgement as opposed to the making of such judgements. Indeed, people who hold profoundly different views about the aesthetic judgement in general may well agree in their judgements about particular works of art. If this is so, would it matter just what account we gave of the aesthetic judgement in general? While it might not matter as far as our day-to-day life goes, and even as far as our day-to-day aesthetic discriminations go, I believe that what we think about the aesthetic judgement in general does have a profound bearing on how we conceive human life in general, and also, by a circuitous route, about how we conceive the value of particular aesthetic objects.

My very strong intuition is that certain responses and evaluations are forced on us (all) by certain works of art: and that this being forced is something which needs explaining, and which cannot be explained so long as we analyse aesthetic response purely in terms of subjective reactions. For if aesthetic response is construed simply in terms of subjective human reactions, without seeing those reactions as reactions to objects which in themselves possess the properties of, e.g. nobility, tragedy, grace, etc., how can we explain the conviction we all at times have that it the objective quality of the work which ought to elicit just that and no other reaction form all well-informed and percipient observers (though which doesn't always do so)?

Beethoven's contemporaries, we feel, largely failed to grasp the spiritual depth, the humour, the lyricism and other qualities of the late quartets. And by this we do not mean just that they were unable to see that later generations would find the quartets spiritually deep, humorous, lyrical, and so on. We mean that (doubtless often for forgivable reasons) they failed to see something which was objectively there, even in 1825; they misperceived the works, misreacted to them, because of their surface strangeness or whatever.

I am assuming in this paper that we all make and understand judgements of the sort I have just made about the late quartets. What I am enquiring into are the conditions of possibility of making such judgements, and I would not expect to carry with me anyone for whom conviction regarding such judgements was not as strong as any other reality in our daily experience (just as one cannot expect to talk fruitfully or seriously about ethics to someone who has never felt obliged to do something right or to refrain from doing something wrong).

Given, though, that we are not Martians or Philistines and do feel both ethical obligation and the essential rightness of certain aesthetic responses, I now want to suggest that two of the most famous accounts of the aesthetic judgement fail to do justice to what presents itself to us (on occasion) as the bindingness and essential correctness of specific judgements. The accounts I have in mind are those of Hume and Kant, and I will begin with Kant, because Kant establishes certain principles and distinctions in the area which are valid, and which I will be assuming in what follows.

For Kant the aesthetic judgement (or what he calls the judgement of taste) is disinterested, universal and nonobjective (in modern philosophical jargon, non-cognitive). By saying that the judgement of taste is disinterested, Kant means that we are not interested in consuming the object we are reacting to; or, more precisely, that our judgement of it is a judgement which prescinds from its consumability. We are interested, Kant says, in 'the real existence of the object', and contemplate it for its own sake, not as something we are about to consume or sell or use. (Hence Kant would distinguish clearly between those elements in an art dealer's evaluation of a work which pertain to the work's saleability and those which pertain to its aesthetic qualities, even if the dealer himself might have problems with making such distinctions). More generally, we might characterise the disinterestedness of the aesthetic judgement in terms of the object in question – and it need not be a work of art – being contemplated rather than used. We can, of course, go on to use something we contemplate aesthetically, and (as we shall see) its fittedness to function could be part of what we admire about it aesthetically. But, in making an aesthetic judgement, we look at the object and its various qualities (including perhaps its functionality) in a disinterested way, and not in terms of any use we might be about to make of it.

While he denies the real existence of any specifically aesthetic property in making a judgement of taste, Kant does not take us in making such judgements to be expressing purely personal preferences. We intend that our judgements about the Beethoven quartets, say, or about Turner's paintings should be universally accepted. It is not like me saying that I can't stand cream soda and my children loving it, whereas I do think that there is something seriously lacking in the taste (judgement) of the man who cannot recognise the qualities of Beethoven's music or of Turner's painting.

Kant also makes a distinction between pure and dependent beauty, pure beauty being found where the free play of the imagination and the understanding delights in purposeless form for its own sake, dependent beauty being where we, in a detached way, rejoice in an object as being particularly fine of its type. The distinction between pure and dependent beauty raises many complicated and interesting questions; for my purposes, though, it will be enough to say that in Kant's account it opens the door – to put it no stronger – to the possibility that taste and aesthetic judgement need not be concerned solely with what is beautiful in some formal sense, detached from other humanly relevant considerations. It means that even though we may wish to maintain a distinction between the aesthetic and the moral, say, or the aesthetic and the functional, the disinterestedness of the aesthetic judgement need not imply that in making properly aesthetic discriminations we are barred from introducing considerations drawn from the moral, the functional and the human generally. Let me put it like this: I may be greatly taken by the technical quality – brilliance of line, draughtsmanship, etc. – of a work and its inventive imaginativeness – and still be unhappy with its human content, its lack of nobility, say. Referring to the lack of nobility in a Bacon portrait would be relegated to being part of a judgement of dependent beauty by Kant because we can judge its absence as being important only against some notion of a perfect man, but it would still, for me as for Kant, be part of the aesthetic discrimination of the object. Indeed, I would part company here with Kant and speculate that most aesthetic judgements take us beyond the purely formal qualities of a work and take us into a realm in which notions of human flourishing and well-being have a role to play, and so, in Kant's terms, have dependent beauty as their focus.

Kant's next mark of the aesthetic judgement is that such judgements are characteristically singular; that is, they are single judgements about single objects. Aesthetic judgements, then, require acquaintance with the particular object or objects in question and cannot be reduced to or explained in terms of general rules. This point of Kant's will doubtless command widespread assent from artists, who rightly insist that acquaintance with the object is essential and cannot in the case of a painting or a sculpture, say, be replaced by a photograph. But one might speculate that this emphasis on the particular and singular nature of the object of the aesthetic judgement, and the judgement's irreducibility to rule or to formal algorithm could well be a strong factor in getting many people to sympathise with Kant's claim that the aesthetic judgement is not objective.

Science and its methods have such a grip on our imagination that, despite all the evidence that we have to the contrary from daily life and from the everyday use of language, we find it hard to envisage that a judgement could be at the same time not formalisable and objective. And certainly Kant himself saw the aesthetic object as being fundamentally non-objective; that is, he saw it as referring not to qualities of the object to which we are applying various concepts (noble, tragic, graceful, etc.), but rather to the reactions we have to the object. The determining ground of the judgement of taste, he says right at the start of the *Critique of Judgment*, 'can be no other than subjective'. The judgement of taste is not a cognitive judgement; its reference is to feelings of satisfaction or dissatisfaction we have with the object, and we determine the beauty of anything by referring it in imagination to such feelings in ourselves and others.

In analysing aesthetic judgements in terms of human reaction, Kant was following Hume, as he was in finding in such judgements something approaching universality. For Hume, as for Kant, seeing a natural object as beautiful or as (aesthetically) deformed is a matter of 'gilding or staining it with the colours borrowed from internal sentiment'. Nevertheless, Hume is also insistent that

> the same Homer, who pleased at Athens and Rome two thousand years ago, is still admired at Paris and at London. All the changes of climate, government, religion, and language have not been able to obscure his glory. Authority or prejudice may give a temporary vogue to a bad poet or orator; but his reputation will never be durable or general. When his compositions are examined by posterity or foreigners, the enchantment is dissipated and his faults appear in their true colours. On the contrary, a real genius, the longer his works endure, and the more wide they are spread, the more sincere is the admiration which they meet with.

Hume like Kant then, wants to hold both that the aesthetic judgement is potentially universal and that its source and ultimate reference is human taste; both that there is such a thing as good taste, if you like, vindicated and manifested through the test of time, and that this good taste is not warranted by the objects themselves, but is rather a matter of those objects conforming to our mind (gilding and staining) and exists merely in our minds. For Hume, as for Kant, the cross-cultural and trans-temporal critical-creative dialogue which elicits the cool, unprejudiced judgement that – e.g. Homer is a poet of great stature – is ultimately a dialogue about our feelings, not about anything objectively or really there in Homer's lines.

Because I find the attempt in Hume and Kant to subjectivise the aesthetic judgement very hard to accept, especially when such an attempt, as it does in this case, goes along with the potential universality of aesthetic judgements, I want now to suggest an alternative approach, but one which does not deny two crucial features of our system of aesthetic valuation. These features are 1) that this system is based in human response and 2) that it is a value system: that is, it is a system, like morality, in which the individual agent or perceiver feels himself moved, i.e. attracted, or disgusted, or motivated in various ways. It was, of course, these facts that led Hume, Kant and many of their followers to insist that aesthetic and other valuations we make are ultimately non-objective and non-factual.

My position by contrast is, in essence, this. The moral and aesthetic judgements we make are not factual in the scientific sense. That is to say, they are not about things which, in theory at least, do not need any specifically human sensibility to discern or uncover. Nor are they about measurable facts, or properties whose existence can be discerned by application of a rule. But, against Kant and Hume, I want to suggest that there may be disclosures of reality which can only become apparent to perceivers or agents constituted in certain ways, with particular sensory apparatus or structures of feeling and sensibility, and which may even require the unpredictable and unformalisable operation of genius to elicit.

My first point is to insist that just because certain features of the world are apparent only to creatures of a certain type, it does not follow that what they perceive cannot be real or objective, nor a valid disclosure of reality. To assert they cannot will be to make the question-begging assumption that natural science – that study which prescinds from observer relative properties – is to be taken as providing the touchstone of reality and objectivity. Once that is done, of course, morality, aesthetic quality and everything else outside natural science, including perhaps consciousness itself and its contents, become illusions or illusion-generating, of secondary status ontologically and epistemologically.

I concede that I have no knock-down argument against what I have called the question-begging assumption of the foundational nature of natural science, except an appeal to experience – the experience of value and aesthetic quality as real – but in making this concession I would not want it thought that my position has become irremediably weak as against natural science: for in the end, it is only through their conformity to, and explanatory power over, experiences we have and observations we make that we grant the statements of natural science the accolade of objective. And, it seems to me, in their own realms objectivist accounts of both morality and aesthetics conform to and explain central ethical and aesthetic experiences we have in a way subjectivist accounts cannot.

What I mean by talking of an objectivist account of value and of aesthetic judgement is this: that, while our judgements in these areas are our judgements, judgements made possible by our constitution and traditions and, in some cases, by the creations and disclosures of genius, they nevertheless reveal genuine properties of the objects or events or actions in question. When Hume and his followers say that they, on inspecting a murder, say, or a beautiful sunset, can find nothing in what they see that counts as the evil or the beauty in question, they are in fact saying little more than that evil and beauty are not properties which feature in certain types of reductive (scientific) description. But in taking this view, they then have considerable difficulty in explaining either the convergence in such judgements, which they admit, or the manner in which aesthetic judgements on occasion, at least, present themselves to us as authoritative and compelling. On the objectivist view, our moral and aesthetic sensibilities would be regarded as tuning us into something real and just as much there as atoms and molecules, even though (like a radio set) it needs a special type of receiver to pick it up. Moreover the objectivist view, in contrast to the subjectivist one, is not committed to saying that the vast majority of human beings are in error when they believe that, in speaking of a murder being a vicious act or of a sunset as beautiful, they are speaking about properties of the murder or the sunset, as opposed to feelings in their own breasts.

The objectivist view of aesthetic evaluation, which I am adumbrating, not only avoids convicting us all of error and explains our shared sense of the non-arbitrary nature of at least some aesthetic judgements. It also helps to explain why – as both Hume and Kant recognise – experienced, knowledgeable and sensitive judges of works of art who are imbued with an absence of prejudice tend to agree in their judgements; and how the best of these judgements, as taste itself, is trans-temporal and, sometimes, even transcultural. (After all, none of us is a classical Greek or a mediaeval Florentine, and even with small knowledge, most of us can appreciate the fineness of say, Japanese painting or Islamic architecture). When an enquiry is both about something objective and on the right lines, there will tend to be a convergence on the part of disinterested enquirers. And where an enquiry is about real objects, participants in it will concentrate on picking out features of the objects under consideration. This again is a feature of critical discourse, which, at its best, and *pace* Hume, spends more time discussing the qualities of the objects viewed than it does in expressing the critic's feelings about them.

What are the metaphysical consequences of analysing aesthetic judgements in objective terms? In an essay entitled 'Against Dryness', Iris Murdoch wrote:

> We no longer see man against a background of values, of realities which transcend him. We picture man as a brave naked will surrounded by an easily comprehended empirical world. For the hard idea of truth, we have substituted a facile idea of sincerity.

One possible interpretation of the objectivity of aesthetic value would be to see it in terms of a background of values such as Iris Murdoch postulates, of realities which transcend us. The hard idea of truth against which we compare our judgements of Homer, Beethoven, Turner and the rest would be a metaphysical fabric of value, something built into the universe, and which our own aesthetic creations, perceptions, occasionally and fleetingly reveal to us. As Iris Murdoch put it in *The Fire and the Sun*:

Good art, thought of as symbolic force rather than statement, provides a stirring image of a pure transcendent value, a steadily visible enduring higher good, and perhaps provides for many people, in an unreligious age without prayer or sacraments, their clearest experience of something grasped as separate and precious and beneficial and held quietly and unpossessively in the attention.

For a Platonism of this sort the magnetism of aesthetic value would stem not – as it does for Hume and Kant – from the fact that our perceptions of aesthetic value stem from within our breasts; it would rather be that what is within us is itself attracted and pulled to something beyond us, in this case the Beautiful, or the Real under the aspect of the Beautiful.

For most of us, such a thought is too heady and too problematic, despite its echoes in the writings of many of the great artists. And perhaps the objectivity of the aesthetic does not require so grand an edifice in which to dwell. We might say this: against Platonism, it is not the case that the world has been made for us or we for the world. The world does not respond to our feelings and our feelings do not in any significant way give us a key to its inner nature or fabric of value. The initial source of our evaluations, moral and aesthetic, are indeed, as Hume and Kant argue, certain feelings in human beings. (Hence, again, the magnetism of value). But once we, collectively and individually, begin to refine our ethical and aesthetic reactions to things, and to discuss them with each other, we start to think of the things themselves as good or bad, cruel or kind, dignified or noble, beautiful or ugly, and, most important, we begin to envisage the possibility that many, or on occasion, even most people, might be wrong on such matters. At this point, what might have begun as gilding and staining on our part, has gilded and stained the world and the world and its objects are really gilded and stained. To call a musical theme noble is not just to speak about feelings it evokes; it is to draw people's attention to certain features of the theme in a particular way. In such circumstances, aesthetic feeling or reaction may well follow the cognitive analysis, and will in any case be justified in terms of the analysis. In Kantian terms, the aesthete is now judging and cognising, as much as he is legislating. When this point is reached, as from the point of view of the race it was reached millennia ago, a system of 'anthropocentric properties and human responses has surely taken on a life of its own. Civilisation has begun' (David Wiggins, 'Towards a Sensible Subjectivism' in *Needy Values and Truths*. That is, human beings have ceased to be moved merely by animal instincts and idiosyncratic urges, and have begun to see their evaluations as corrigible and decidable on the basis of conversations directing attention to features of the world and its objects. As children, of course, each of us is introduced to conversations of this sort, and our reactions are guided by the criteria implicit in them. In so far as these reactions are world-directed and objective in this way we can see why, even if we do not believe in a transcendent aesthetic realm, it will be the case that aesthetic judgements are made with the intention of commanding universal assent.

We may, of course, wish to ask what sort of creature it is who can generate a system of objective value in this way. But for my purposes today, it is quite enough to raise with you the possibility that the aesthetic might be a realm of objective value. We may conceive this realm in Platonic metaphysical terms, in terms of the deep constitution of the universe, to which we are responding in our judgement of beauty. Or we may conceive it as an aspect of an autonomous form of life brought about initially in response to human tastes and desires (in Kant's terms, 'produced' by them), but then, as a form of life and as a source of human activity and interest, breaking free from particular instances of those tastes and desires to become a realm of objective value against which particular tastes and desires are formed and judged. In either conception we will be attributing to human beings a significant degree of autonomy from the immediacy and tyranny of impulse and desire.

The Canadian Grandmother

MARJORIE ALLTHORPE-GUYTON

Editor, 'Artscribe'

The mechanisms by which art work accrues value, that is, status and monetary worth in the Western art world, have been, superficially at least, quite visible. Imagine a bullseye, like a dartboard, where success is graduated from the centre out: from the studio to final triumph – a show at Castelli, New York and selection for Documenta. This is the field of Willi Bongard's game 'Art and Commerce' which first appeared in the German weekly *Capital* in June 1982.[1] From 1971 until his death in 1985, Dr Willi Bongard, once called 'the most hated man in the German art scene', published his monthly newsletter, *Art Actuell*, charting the shifting fortunes of a 'Top 100' contemporary artists. These were selected on a points system allocated on the achievement of one-person, group shows, critical reviews, etc. There is inevitably a heavy US/German bias accurately reflecting the dominant focus of the so-called international art world of the last two decades. The archive is, as Lauf states, 'an exhaustive spectrum of the art of our time. (Hockney's graph dives downwards – Nauman's shoots straight up.) The twenty year records of price fluctuations alone are worthy of individual study and could yield the type of socioeconomic analysis pioneered by Arnold Hauser, Gerald Reitlinger and Michael Baxandall for other epochs'. Bongard's influence is attested by the satirical artwork by Klaus Staeck 'Stamp of Approval', bearing the image of the heads of Bongard and Harald Szeeman, internationally renowned curator and critic.[2]

Bongard held curators to be 'The Popes of Art' and there is no doubt, as Cornelia Lauf says, that Willi Bongard legitimated 'a cadre of largely white, largely male artists on the basis of their financial and institutional clout'. He was also extraordinarily prescient of the wholesale and unapologetic embrace of the market which gained momentum throughout the 1980s and now seems to have ground to a perplexing halt. A situation brought about largely by recession but also I believe by a feeling of bankruptcy, not so much financial (although that is real enough for many) but spiritual. In 1981 Bongard could write and be applauded for his convictions 'It is my primary goal to convince you that manipulation is needed. By this I mean manipulation in the sense of acting, caring, taking matters into one's hands in order to make art happen and to endow it with meaning and economic value. To achieve this, it seems to me that in principle any means is justified and any path is right because after love, art is the most important thing in the world'.

In 1991 those means and ends are coming under fierce scrutiny as the aesthetic dimension is fractured and the walls of the White Cube breached by the imperative of a socially engaged art, art with real purpose, art that is of use. In the 1980s meaning and economic value became conflated, meaning no longer endowed value but was contingent to it or was drained away altogether. A so-called postmodernist strategy that earned high reputations, and which Jeremy Gilbert-Rolfe characterised as 'entirely complacent, such works offer an equally predictable criticality, and it is a criticality which is emptied of meaning by virtue of its taking place in the gallery or the museum'.[3] In 1987 Willi Bongard's archive was bought by the Getty Centre for the History of Art and the Humanities, Los Angeles.

To turn to the Canadian Grandmother... Joyce Knapp cooked 'Strange, unorthodox meals for her friends and family, especially her husband: Sculpted Meat, a large cylindrical rissole of minced veal stuffed with eleven different kinds of cooked vegetables. This cylinder, standing upright in the middle of the plate is crowned with a thick layer of honey and supported at the bottom by a sausage ring which rests on three golden spheres of chicken meat. Joyce's food had meaning alright, but in what context? A neat, unassuming woman in her early sixties, at the end of her first term as a member of the MA Fine Art course at Goldsmiths' College she received two external examiners in her kitchen set up in a small room off the gallery. They were offered cookies in the shape of letters and words, household names. Joyce liked to cook the News. And what was this? A homely parodic array of familiar words in chocolate biscuit, in capital letters: IRONY, DECONSTRUCTION, DESIRE. Joyce had cooked the course. Very good. On close questioning, however, it became clear that Joyce Knapp was not at all seduced by theory, she decided early on that she did not need it; she simply held the conviction that what she did and had always done, every day, was art. It needed no justification, nor even an extended life. She expected her work to be eaten, even the special cakes she had buried in the garden. It was not important to her to discover that there was a theoretical context for her 'practice'. She was not eager to meet Sylvia Ziranik or Bobby Baker, neither did she wish to acquaint herself with their North American sisters. Although later, in her seminar paper, she took great interest in the manifesto of Futurist cookery. 'They were trying to expand sensual appreciation in all areas with exuberance at the table and the bed. They enjoyed the encounter with unusual combinations of foods. They embraced with enthusiasm all that is new, striving to liberate language, art and life from tradition and convention. All human experience is liberated by the availability of art in everyday life. Art and life are not separate. Ordinary, everyday activities should be carried out with flair and enthusiasm.'[4] Joyce did not seem this articulate at the end of that first term. She received a warning.

The problem of Joyce Knapp had given rise to some arduous soul-searching and some perplexed and tortuous discussion on the objectives of the course, on questions of value, on the autonomy of art. The opening night of her degree show, in which she played a live part, was her hour of triumph: a young artist from elsewhere exclaimed 'That student who hired the grandmother is brilliant'. And what had she actually produced? A luncheon menu of food palindromes, a few jars of 'Braising Sauce', a cookie carbohydrate chain and the Canadian Grandmother badge, factory-made bearing her newly minted brand name. The Canadian Grandmother had a corporate image.

What Joyce Knapp stubbornly proclaimed, with not a little Duchampian wit, was no more and no less than the undermining of that distinction between art and life, between public and private, which is the core of a classical aesthetic tradition and which has hardly been shifted by the self-reflexive positions of work underpinned by postmodernist irony and indeterminacy. In many ways her ideas about art echo those of Allan

Kaprow who in the late 1950s joined John Cage's New School for Social Research along with Claes Oldenberg and Dick Higgins. David Hughes wrote in 1989 about his encounter with Kaprow: 'he had prepared a number of events to be filmed. Prolific as ever, he urged us through a crammed itinerary of interviews to camera, and activities in a forest, his in-laws' kitchen and on Clacton beach. Not to mention a pub lunch which seemed to be the highlight of his day, his constant preoccupation all morning and a sub-text to our conversations. Cage is also obsessed with food – his texts are full of references to it.'[5] After cleaning the kitchen floor using Q-tips and his own spit, Kaprow 'talked constantly of the stories the floor told him of the life of the kitchen and its occupants ... He wanted to let life, once thought of as an annoyance, the enemy of art, into the domain of art. This opening up of art brought the charge of "impurity". At first he thought it an insult, but then he thought: "Well, that's a marvellous thing, to be impure."'

It is the example of Allan Kaprow that Suzi Gablik invokes to support the main argument of her recently published book *The Re-enchantment of Art* (1991).[6] 'In a provocative essay called "The Real Experiment", Kaprow maintains there have always been two traditions going on simultaneously within modernism: "artlike" art (in which art is separated from life and everything else) and "lifelike" art (in which art is connected to life and everything else). It has been artlike art, according to Kaprow, that had predominantly occupied the attention of artists and public, and that is seen as the most serious part of the mainstream Western art-historical tradition. This art engages in dialogue with other art, and is supported by galleries, museums and professional art journals, all of whom, he says, need artists whose art is artlike'.[7]

It is the endlessly repeated theme of Gablik's book that the dominant modernist aesthetic is complicit, indeed is the vehicle of a Cartesian view of the world which is proven to be so destructive as to be no longer sustainable. It is a thesis which is well rehearsed, particularly in a little known study *The Death of Nature, Women, Ecology and the Scientific Revolution* by an American historian of science, Carolyn Merchant (1980).[8] Gablik does not refer to this work in her bibliography. To be fair, her book is a meditation on art and the world, it is not a scholarly discourse and there are lengthy descriptions of the activities of artists who recognise that a new agenda is in order and that art must be on it, that art must engage, not distance itself from society. A Kantian aesthetic, where, as Terry Eagleton puts it 'facts are one thing, and values another ... where we ascribe to an object a felt harmony of our own creative powers',[9] is no longer supportable because it is precisely those powers of the centred subject that have resulted not only in the loss of meaning 'in an increasingly rationalised, secularised, demythologised environment' but in the destruction of that environment. Gablik insists we no longer want art where the chief source of value is the object. 'I suspect we are at the end of something – a hypermasculinized modern culture whose social projects have become increasingly unecological and nonsustainable'.[10] She calls for a total revision of what it means to be a 'successful' artist in the world today: 'the challenge of the future will be to transcend the disconnectedness and separation of the aesthetic from the social that existed within modernism' ... 'modern aesthetics has been coloured by a kind of compulsive masculinity and I don't just mean in the sense that, at least for Greenberg, art history seems to consist entirely of male walruses'.

If Gablik constantly overstates what is undoubtedly a compelling case it is because she is attempting to break the 'one philosophical framework we have'. To break the mould of what she categorises as a 'value-free' art. (Grist to her mill would be Antonin Artaud's strangely potent statement: '*The Grid* is a terrible moment for substance and sensitivity').

Her targets are predictable: Richard Serra with the 'Tilted Arc' is the High Priest of autocratic and irresponsible modernism and David Salle and Allan McCollum are the Masters of the Act of Disappearance, who make work 'where the "will" to meaning often deliberately courts meaninglessness and even finds satisfaction in it.' Their perpetual deconstruction of modernist languages she sees as a temporary entertainment which has palled. There is little doubt that their games are beginning to assume as much closure as their modernist models: 'We no longer need old authoritarian ideologies, which demand that art be difficult, wilfully inaccessible and disturbing to the audience – in some sense a contest of wills – as it was under modernism.'

Gablik's imperative calls in effect for a total negation of the way in which value judgments have been made in contemporary art. This does not just entail the kind of thing James Turrell meant when he said 'For me art isn't something you carry up to an East Side Manhattan apartment in an elevator',[11] 'it is pilgrimage to some remote place to experience art in what are now for us unknown cosmic conditions'. What Suzi Gablik wants is for artists to abandon the studio, the gallery, the art fair, to walk with the world, to selflessly, like Mother Teresa, help the needy, the spiritually and materially bereft. She seems to forget that artists tend to suffer poverty more than most. Her main objective is ecologically purposeful art, art with use-value, art which does not set itself apart from a social order which dispossesses people and destroys the earth. In short an emancipatory art, offering models of reconciliation which embody a clear Marxist aesthetic where the commodity is the antithesis of the aesthetic object, but also allowing for a receptive, feminine aesthetic where the production of things is not necessarily the means to ends.

'Art also pollutes, consumes the world. What about self erasure in art – art that cleans up after itself? (Robert Janz).[12] Or art that ceases to exist in material form at all? The problem with the alternative art which Gablik introduces is that its rituals and 'empowerment ceremonies' in the name of Gaia may be deeply rewarding for the artist, but to the onlooker they still seem self indulgent, even risible. It is hard not to suppress a giggle at the outfit of Fern Shaffer undertaking her 'Crystal Clearing, Winter Solstice' 1986. More importantly, Gablik is narrowly focused in her research of alternative practices, she makes no mention of British initiatives since the 1960s, notably APG (Artist Placement Group) where artists John Latham, Stuart Brisley and Ian Breakwell among others worked in communities and institutions as enablers and advisors with no requirement to produce art objects. (Although she does acknowledge her glaring omission of the subject of cultural diversity, which is tackled by Lucy Lippard in her new book *Mixed Blessings: New Art in a Multicultural America*). The main weakness of Gablik's book is her simplistic treatment of the question of art and morality. She does not deal adequately with the complexities of the uncoupling in modernity of art from the cognitive, the ethical and the political which Eagleton deals with, with such rigour and humour. She does not adequately investigate one of the overriding problems of contemporary art practice: its apparent cynicism of which Jeff Koons is the exemplar. She advocates the drawing together of life and art but does not recognise fully the ethical and moral problems this can provoke. We continue to value Jeff Koons because we are still in thrall to our culture, still fascinated by a pornography of excess and seduced by spectacles of power. There is just a remote possibility that lean times will bring about that sea change at the heart of Duchamp's project. 'I hope that this mediocrity conditioned by too many factors extraneous to art per se will this time lead to an ascetic order, of which the general public will not even be aware, and that only a few of the initiated will develop on the margin of a world blinded by the fireworks of economics.'[13]

If this still sounds like an elitist male position, an expression of an aesthetics of indifference, so be it. Art is, must be, amoral, its illuminations neither sacred nor profane.

Notes

1. See Cornelia Lauf, 'Snakes and Ladders, The Archive of Dr. Willi Bongard', *Artscribe*, no.84, Nov./Dec. 1990, pp.67–71.
2. Ibid. repr. pp.70–1.
3. Jeremy Gilbert-Rolfe, 'The Price of Goodness', *Artscribe*, no.78, Nov./Dec. 1989, p.50.
4. Joyce Knapp, 'Futurist Banquets Past and Present', second year seminar paper, MA Fine Art 1991.
5. David Hughes, 'Tell-Tale Art', *Artscribe*, no.81, May 1990, pp.11–12.
6. Suzi Gablik, *The Re-enchantment of Art*, London 1991.
7. Ibid., p.137.
8. Carolyn Merchant, *The Death of Nature: Women, Ecology and the Scientific Revolution* (USA 1980, Great Britain 1982).
9. Terry Eagleton, 'The Kantian Imaginary', *The Ideology of the Aesthetic*, Oxford 1990.
10. Gablik 1991 and following quotations.
11. Ibid., p.83.
12. Ibid., p.91.
13. Marcel Duchamp, Philadelphia conference 1961 quoted by Liz Brooks, 'Marcel Waves', *Artscribe*, no.90, Feb./March 1992, p.76.

Confronting the canvas – in the studio and in the tutorial room

PAUL HUXLEY

Professor of Painting, The Royal Collage of Art

I am an artist and head of a postgraduate painting school. If I were in another profession I could plead innocence and say that I have been kicked upstairs but the truth is that nobody can be blamed for kicking me here.

So, like many an artist who teaches, I spend time conducting administration when, in fact, I made my reputation painting pictures. And I examine students' work, making value judgements on subjects I hold so dear to my heart that I do not wish to see them diminished in stature by the process of definition. Perhaps that is why I persist in doing it.

Like most professionals, my social world is limited to like-minded people. Only rarely, say two or three times a year, do I meet that nasty question, 'Teach art? – surely not! After all what is good or bad is a matter of personal opinion isn't it?'

I have even once or twice failed a student. Can I sleep at night in the knowledge of what must be a wide body of common lore that says that all judgement is merely subjective? Elsewhere I am on record for promoting an opposite view. 'Art', I said, 'not only can be taught but must be taught.' In my support, I invoked the works of John Constable who said, 'A self-taught artist is one taught by a very ignorant person!' I went on to say: 'that people are born with talent is unquestioned, but it should be made clear that, as in the case of writers or composers, dancers or actors, talent must be trained by constant practice, informed by the great achievement of others and challenged with intellectual rigour so as to nurture its continuing development. Painting is not a mere act of physical dexterity; it is first a statement of the intellect, and as such it is perceived and understood'.

To an extent this emphasis is recognised in art schools today, but I need to put it in context. Very few art schools existed before the mid-nineteenth century except for the Royal Academy Schools, where, incidentally, I studied. Previously most teaching was along the age-old lines of master and apprentice relationships. The Industrial Revolution brought a backlash of social concern for the education of the underprivileged, and also a concern to ensure that that which could be industrially produced should also have the humanising qualities of decoration, taste and style associated with handcrafted artifacts, the qualities that could only be designed into the product by artists. Victorian art schools blossomed and they tended to believe that the best and most universal training was through an approach similar to that for a fine artist. That is, to learn the history of Classic forms, to observe and analyse structure and proportion in nature by copying and by drawing from observation, and to develop the skills to recreate from knowledge and memory.

This was largely my art school training in the early 1950s, when it was still possible to enter art school at the age of thirteen and learn the ABC of art through anatomy, perspective, the history of ornament and architecture, drawing from life and figure composition. These were the stepping stones towards learning to speak in a language through the medium of paint on canvas. Thirteen is an appropriate age to loose one's innocence in many ways. The average child seems to draw and paint wonderfully until he or she is old enough to know better. Then they give up in despair. At that age a child can welcome the challenge of a disciplined classical training where the goals are relatively easy to recognise and standards measured.

In the 1960s William Coldstream and his committee made a report which effected change. Maybe he thought that there had been too much emphasis on craft and skill and that intellect was being undervalued. Maybe he even saw that the acceleration of technology together with the burgeoning quantity of recent art history and theory demanded more mature minds. Certainly he saw that art schools would not receive a fair share of the public purse in the future unless they became academically respectable and awarded something like a degree. The advice was taken and as a consequence we probably benefited a great deal more than we were harmed.

The result was that students became older and better qualified academically. More than ever before courses had to be constructed that took account of theory as well as skill. Students have to be assessed on their creative making as well as the reason for its making. A case is argued for establishing a basis for making judgements of artistic value.

The new arrival at art school is more sophisticated today than before but less skilled. At eighteen she will already know from television that Jackson Pollock threw paint, that Andy Warhol traced round photographs, that Marcel Duchamp just made choices and that a number of artists with considerable cachet from Yves Kline onwards appear often to have ideas but do nothing at all with their hands. The student will be very resistant to the grinding discipline which was once the only source of invention.

I won't meet this student for another few years so let me leave her waiting for her tutorial and return to my studio. I have earlier argued that art is of the head more than of the hand. But how often do I relearn after a fallow period or an enforced time spent away from painting when I excuse myself by saying 'I'm working it out in my head', that back in the studio one eventually continues at exactly the point where one left off. An imagined work is always defied by its manifestation.

It is courage not mere expediency that teaches you, as the scaffolding for the grand concept is put into place, that it won't do, and that perhaps an incidental by-product will provide the key to what you are really after. Because what we are seeking is at first a figment of the imagination and has no manifest form until we meet it face to face and recognise it. Science and art are not so different here.

Breakthrough in scientific fields is usually recognised to be made by a creative or imaginary leap which is then substantiated, rather than through logical deduction. And again, how often have I proved the value of thinking aloud with a pen or pencil, externalising thoughts before rejecting them even when the thought seems unworthy of record. Because only when the idea takes physical shape do we know its real nature and potential. One act leads to another by comparison and rejection, extension and mutation.

Ideas from the mind direct what the hand makes but what becomes visible feeds the imagination of the mind. Put in a parallel way – the old concept of Homo sapiens inventing tools because he was intelligent is discredited in favour of the view that he used tools and thereby became intelligent.

A painting evolves by comparisons. A mark against a surface where no mark exists, a colour against another which alters its value. Elements have qualities in relation to their context. The quality of one work in relation to other works and these eventually placed in the context of society and history. Ideally, a work of art will carry the clues by which it should be read within itself. A work of art can reveal in what way it is a work of art as well as revealing what it has to say within that mode. Also possibly it is the nature of art, paradoxically to demonstrate itself as art in the face of not being what we always thought art was.

But I should be warned by Wittgenstein here when he said 'No representation can fully contain the means by which it represents'. This has been popularly explained by the example of a map, perhaps showing the route through London to this building. For the map to show in what way it represents London it might require an aerial perspective drawing linking the features. But then the drawing will need some explanation which shows on what basis linear perspective is projected, and so on ad infinitum. Wittgenstein must be right. Our information is encoded and the holders of the cipher are those living within a shared culture.

The student has waited long enough and it is time to leave my studio for the tutorial room. She is one of the privileged few who have reached a postgraduate school. Is this a case of the survival of the fittest? When Darwin used that phrase he didn't mean fit in the sense of physical fitness but fit in the Victorian meaning of the word, being fitting for the circumstances. By what process of selection did she get here – natural or otherwise? No – it is not just that she fought off the opposition and found more food for herself, although God knows, among students to this day that remains a factor. The opposition, and I don't mean competition – is outside growling at the door. Demanding conformity to race and creed, to the standards set by what is known, not to rock the boat, nor to probe the conscience of the machinery that drives our society.

Why is she deserving of special protection and encouragement? Why is she considered fit for these circumstances?

She might well have started an undergraduate course four years ago with little more than an invitation to pitch her tent and make a start. A young student's allegiances will be to recent art where there is something to identify with, rather than with the daunting great works of the distant past. But given the bewildering and complex range of movements and counter-movements in this century a student may well take fright. It is one thing to study art history, but it is another to feel, however mistakenly, that one has unwittingly elected to become a player. A typical response is to withdraw into a stylistic nook which preferably does not compete with the neighbours and can be defended when under attack as being a deeply authentic personal language. The more aggressive the intruder the more insistent is the claim that there is a key for deciphering but it is out of reach. Forgivable as this stance is for someone at pains to give birth to a fragile dream, our student has greater gifts and greater potential than that.

She has listened to contradictory advice, questioned it, and tried taking some of it. She has read, and looked at, and listened to, accounts of the history of her discipline but has probably learned her own version of it backwards from those contemporary works with which she identified to their precursors and their precursors' ancestors and all the related tributaries of music literature and philosophy. She has looked at the art which leaves her cold as well as the art for which she has a passion, because she knows there is something of value to be learnt from all. She might have glimpsed the necessity to learn how to be both self-confident and self-critical and to identify her strengths so as not to destroy them and her failings so as to mend them. Above all, she has spent most of her time with pencil or brush in her hand, drawing and painting – observing, testing, comparing, matching, copying, adjusting, imagining, shaping, measuring, obscuring, illuminating, describing, inventing, destroying – and starting all over again. What she has done now is still not good enough. To be effective art must communicate. That isn't to say that is what it's for or that when it succeeds it can be translated.

The rules of engagement suggest that the trap needs bait. For painting to lodge its presence in our lives it needs a hook to entangle us – even if we are unaware that it is there or that it dissolves the moment we identify it as such. The intrigue develops from there through information or misinformation, attracting or repelling, seducing or attacking, concealing or revealing. It is a two way dialogue with the observer.

In the tutorial one tries to translate this dialogue. To peel back the layers of response describing each. Here they can be matched with what the student intended. A comparison can be made between what the painter thinks she's done and how others respond. A painting viewed in the tutorial seems to have a secret language of symbols which are untranslatable. The student agrees, they are invented and with no meaning, the clues are false. Is this wilful mystification a fault to be criticised or is that unfair? After all, is it not possible that we make art according to how we understand art. If art is mysterious to us then we build mystery into our art. The experience of grappling with the puzzle might be integral to the experience, after all, are we not capable of finding meaning in all things if we have a will to do so? Of course, if the result is demonstrably futile the ensuing response will be measured accordingly.

To measure requires objectivity which means a detachment from the threads of our emotional and intellectual make-up. Ultimate objectivity, if that were possible, must cause a detachment so foreign that no communication is possible. The first audience is the artist, the second her friend or wider circle of friends or the imagined mentor, maybe even her teacher. Then the wider audience, those people who share a local culture whether in space or time or strata of society. An artist is local before being 'international'. A great work of art is measured as such by a curious complex of the size, the expertise and the longevity of its audience. Of course, art is subjective and the perceptions and evaluations of it are so too. There is no true objectivity – evaluation is always subjective, but nevertheless measurable within the context of the culture in which it is made.

I would like to add a footnote: one day a few years back my steps took me to the British Museum, not this time just to browse, but enthused by the words of a scientist. The wonderful poetic entomologist, Jean Henri Fabre wrote on the subject of the ancient Egyptians' worship of the Scarab. He describes how the sacred dung beetle feasts on manna dropped from Heaven. How it rolls between its forelegs a ball of camel dung: a replica of the world. The Egyptians carved their own replicas of the sacred beetle with magical hieroglyphics on the underside. To my amazement a printed card beside the exhibit mentioned how scholars had failed to decipher the code, ending with the words 'Although these inscriptions appear to carry information they are now thought to be meaningless'.

A NASA spacecraft has finished skimming the surface of the moons of Jupiter and Saturn and wheels on into outer space beyond the pull of our solar system. Do we know what message we send our fellow intelligences in the universe? We are shown an inscribed plaque, perhaps engraved platinum, or some more durable substance, depicting to our eyes and understanding a diagram of our solar system. No doubt the planetary orbits are faithfully measured and proportionally true. But will the signifying mark that shows our planet earth to be the important one, the source of this message, be understood? And what about these arabesque lines to one side? I can't say which side because I don't know which way up it will be perceived. Viewed a certain way round and once again to our eyes and understanding they depict two human beings, a man and woman. They are naked, the man bearded, the woman's hair long and straight, the man's gently styled a bit like a sixties designer. They stand posed like Adam and Eve in a German Renaissance engraving, perhaps by Durer, or an anatomic diagram derived from it.

Here all association with high art dissolves. The outline presumably attempts to describe volume but it is superficial and inept. Perhaps it means to describe anatomy – but no, the information judging for example our most vital parts, the sexual genitals, is insufficient and coy. To my mind, an Aboriginal bark painting would be far more informative of our culture. But then I am being subjective. The targeted audience, on the other hand, might be the most objective we can hope to contact. What they see (if they have eyes) might give them cause to hesitate. But I suspect they will eventually attach this label which I shall have to translate for you.

Although these inscriptions appear to carry information they are now thought to be meaningless.

The intrinsic relation between the artist and his or her work

ANA MARIA PACHECO
Artist

When I received the final version of the programme for this conference, to my surprise what appeared below my name was not as previously stated, simply 'Artist', but 'painter – formerly Head of Fine Art'. This might seem to be an irrelevant detail; however it does illustrate something rather interesting in relation to what is the object of this debate: 'Judgment and Value'. Why the change? Could it be that just being an artist would not be enough for the specific subject of the discussion, that there was a need to infer a 'better value' to give more credibility to the speaker? I do not know.

I am not going to present my paper as a head of fine art as I prefer to talk in the present tense. Also, the Norwich School of Art, where I worked, no longer exists. Now it has in its place a grandiose establishment called 'The Norfolk Institute of Art and Design'. Far more valuable I am sure!

Today the field of discourse on value is vast. It is a well-ploughed one by a great number of eminent theoreticians. There is no attempt here to emulate them. I will give you my personal view and the basis from which I make judgements on my own work. I think it is important to convey some idea of my background in order to show the roots of my work – it is only in a cultural context that one can make any judgement of one's work – values implied are not autonomous.

Coming from a multi-racial culture, from an early age I had to deal with what has been described as the 'incommensurabilities of modern cultural life'. In Brazil, all the various ages of history seem to co-exist together – primitive peoples, medieval rulers, enormous industrial cities, ascendant bourgeoisie, refined aristocracy, the instability of the workers and a landscape that is unchanged from the time the world was created. The Brazilian culture is full of dilemma, characteristic of a country colonised by Europeans. The historian, Vivien Schelling, points out some of these aspects:

1. Culture Duality
The European culture transplanted to a social and geographical context that was entirely different. It established itself as the dominant and official culture, while the Amerindian and African (imported from the slave trade) cultures were marginalised as 'barbaric'.

When in the 18th century French and English culture replaced Portugal and Spain as centres of European civilization, the Iberian culture was rejected by the Brazilian elite. They then adopted the movements of Europe: baroque, classicism, romanticism and realism. Brazilians had no corresponding social transformation, and had to face a prevalent discrepancy between representation and reality.

Consequences

Appearance and reality. The pervasive sense of contradiction between European and (now North American) institutions and Brazilian reality has had a tremendous repercussion not only for cultural but for political and economic life in the country. The lack of cohesiveness between norms and institutions, as one could argue, created a particular structure of feeling in Brazilian society, characterised by a sensibility to paradox, ambiguity and duplicity. A sensibility to the existence of chaos under the appearance of order, to the comic in the tragic and the tragic in the comic, which is expressed in particular in popular art.

2. *Transculturation*

This term was coined first by the Cuban writer, Fernando Ortiz, in the 1840's to describe the way in which European culture is transformed through its fusion with indigenous culture. It is not just a passive process of acculturation.'

But to me this 'fusion' is only superficial because when Schelling talks about 'cannibalism', referring to the modernist movement in Brazil with its 'cannibalist manifesto', she states:

> Beneath the repressive culture transported to Brazil with the Jesuits and their catechism of the Indians, lies a pagan reality: the Last Supper of Christ is a highly sublimated version of cannibalism … in taking this metaphor further, the sardonic, critical and grotesque vision of human relations as a mutual devouring, points to the true nature of human relations in Brazil.

The work reflects what I am, in an existential condition. In the work, through the interaction between artist and work, there will be a revelation of a 'pre-theoretical' knowledge and a set of background conditions which are saturated with values, convictions and the inevitable contradictions.

Umberto Eco conveys with great clarity and intellectual incisiveness the contradiction implied in creativity:

> it reveals to us that our personality is disassociated, that our possibilities are complementary, that our grasp of reality is subject to contradictions, and that our attempt to define the totality of things and to dominate them is always in certain measure a checkmate.

I feel that being away from my own culture has helped me to develop a more differentiated world view, a differentiated value language; far from attempting to unify all the disparities of my cultural roots but learning how to live with it.

I shall end with a brief observation about art education. In my view the demise of the artist as a person within the art education establishment is a great loss. In a world bankrupt of political ideas, is it safer to put aside the contradictions of creativity? Perhaps the only way to heal this wound is to take the challenges of our time, to take responsibility for our own actions and to deal with the issues raised through contemporary theoretical debate, the deconstruction of political and historical myths, without ever losing sight of our humanity, which should be the regulator of any debate.

[77]

Coming to terms with values

Michael Ginsborg

Artist and teacher, Wimbledon School of Art

I have called this paper 'coming to terms with values' for the fairly obvious reason that, for some considerable time, artistic values have been highly disputed rather than given. Many artists and students, do seem to settle early and conclusively for working values which give consistent direction to their life in art, or career if you prefer. Others do not, and when asking and re-asking questions of meaning and quality, receive answers that seem, at best, provisional. It is a continuing dilemma, in which the procession of ideas, criticism, and analysis on the one hand, and the aura of the art work, ineffable yet specific, on the other, seem to be in a constant state of non-reconciliation.

I would have thought that some consideration of meaning, whether analytical or speculative, some interpretive momentum at work, would have to be an essential part of the judgement of works of art – one's own or others. But in the essay 'Complaints of an Art Critic' of 1967, Clement Greenberg seems to be wrenching aesthetic judgement away from thinking. 'Aesthetic judgements', he says, 'are given and contained in the immediate experience of art. They coincide with it. They are not arrived at afterwards through reflection or thought: you can no more choose whether or not to like a work of art than you can choose to have sugar taste sweet or lemons sour'. He locates the moment of aesthetic judgement in the functions (I can't call them faculties) of sensation and feeling.

In 1984, in an interview with Charles Harrison, Greenberg elaborated. Harrison asked: 'The work of art is identified for you in terms of your response to it. That response is supposedly involuntary and disinterested. It is a special kind of experience. What sets the conditions of relevance to the response? What decides its status as aesthetic?' Greenberg replied: 'When it comes to aesthetic experience you're all alone to start and end with. Other people's responses may put you under pressure but what you then have to do is go back and look again, listen again, read again. You can only modify your aesthetic judgement by re-experiencing. You don't change your mind on reflection. You may get doubts but you have to go back and check again. It's not a matter of probative demonstration. When you can demonstrate an aesthetic judgement probatively art will cease – art as we've known it so far.'

Why has Greenberg's rhetoric been taken so seriously and why have these not entirely new ideas taken hold so strongly in art and art school practice? I think it's not just because he occupied such a central position in American art criticism. What holds such a powerful appeal is the pre-eminence he gives to the gut reaction part of the process and to the individual – 'You're all alone to start and end with' – with your immediate experience. It is a heady mixture, offering independence and exclusivity. But he's not just saying that. He's saying that there is another, non-instinctual part – 'look again, listen again, read again, check again'. The viewer is required to tread a path between thinking and feeling and is subject to all the conflicts and tensions of that passage.

Greenburg said 'When it comes to aesthetic experience you're all alone to start and end with.' What is that 'all alone'? What does it consist of? Psychology has an awful lot to say about it – Greenberg keeps relatively quiet.

Ernst Gombrich, in a recent collection of essays, states that in order to get involved at all, there must be an element of 'initial readiness' and being primed by our culture to expect a rewarding experience. 'Without a readiness to respond', he says, 'or, to use a chilling psychological term, a willingness to project, the work of art will remain inert'. Actually, you can't will projection. It is an unconscious, automatic process whereby a content that is unconscious to the subject transfers itself to an object.

How many times have we been in front of art, on our own, with colleagues, or with students and felt and said things like 'That's an incredibly uplifting painting, a buoyant celebratory painting, or a tragic or anguished painting'. These are reactions we own, not the painting. The work of art activates these feelings in us. It doesn't possess them. We do. The artist might have done.

Greenberg leaves us well before this point. It is a psychological point. Later in 'Complaints of an Art Critic' Greenberg says of Edvard Munch: 'I know of nothing in art that affects me in anything like the way that his literature does, yet the purely pictorial impact of his art remains something else. Compared, say with Matisse, Munch never looks more than minor. How then does his illustration manage to carry so strongly and convey so intensely?' I would suggest that the answer lay with Greenberg looking at what he was projecting onto Munch's imagery. However, he *has* made a judgement.

Matisse bowls him over in the eye more than Munch. Munch, however, bowls him over emotionally. He's uncomfortable with it, but he's decided. I'm not happy with it either, because it maintains the traditional antinomy of form and content. Munch has form too and Matisse has content – which is only the content it is because it is in the form it is in. However, I don't really want to dwell on the interests at work in Greenberg's formalist polemic and critical practice. Rather, I want to look at the implications of the protected space Greenberg has been misunderstood as offering, a space which limits critical dialogue rather than allowing for a dialectical relationship with it. A space in which artistic judgements are innate rather than acquired, a space which privileges the unconscious yet rarely names it.

Terry Atkinson has written somewhere, or he has said, that 'The theory that practice has nothing to do with theory is a theory, a disingenuous and naive one but nonetheless a theory'. What are the antecedents of this naive and disingenuous theory? In very general terms only, one could posit two very broad, interdependent tendencies in current artistic practice. They should certainly not be taken as exclusive, and for me at any rate, the distinction, such as it is, is not a qualitative one.

In the first, critical discourse is not only admitted into the arena of practice, it is seen as constituting it. The 'visual' for its own sake is eschewed – actually it's not even a possibility, except as an ironic quote, because the visual is seen as one part of a broad cultural field and not only capable of addressing, but in fact, obliged to address political, critical, or ideological issues. Art practice is seen as a deconstructive enquiry into the nature of the artistic institution. This tendency is seen as stemming from the work of Marcel Duchamp, amongst others. In the second tendency the values at work are very different. Intuition, discovery and spontaneity are the priorities. The eye is what is important. Practices such as music, dance and poetry are seen as usefully analogous to visual art. Verbal articulation and criticism are secondary in the face of the visual practice itself – unless, that is, they deal with form, technique, or process.

It is tempting to be mischievous here and say that those in the first group use various different media and those in the second group are usually painters, or that those in the first group are cold fish, whereas those in the second group are passionate, and so on and so forth, but it simply isn't so.

The values at work in that second tendency derive in a recent and general way from the end of the last century and the beginning of this one, and more specifically we can understand them by looking at Cézanne and at Matisse, who regarded Cézanne as a master. Here, the artist's work is conceived of as a search for the kind of synthesis that only the artist can make. Cézanne, both in the work and in the image of the artist, is seen as evidence of this search. The later paintings are experienced simultaneously as representations of the motif and as representations of the process of finding that representation. Matisse distinguished Cézanne's work as 'moments of the artist', in contrast to Sisley's which he called 'moments of nature'. Or, as Richard Shiff puts it in his excellent book *Cézanne and the End of Impressionism*: 'Sisley depicts nature, Cézanne represents himself'.

Artistic practice is seen as the search for origins which (and I'm quoting from Richard Shiff again) 'can be understood as absolutes that are neither part of, derived from, nor dependent on anything else.' Here I think lies something of the root of Greenberg's dictum 'When it comes to aesthetic experience you're all alone to start and end with.' Shiff goes on: 'Origins could be nature, self, or perhaps an encompassing deity and the aspiration to reach them constituted the absolute goals of art. The artist who discovers something true about nature or himself cannot be accused of deception, for he cites an unimpeachable source – the artist who makes such a discovery is seen as authentic.'

'Original' in this context is not meant in the colloquial sense as 'different' but as origin, a point back beyond which the work cannot be taken. The essence, as it were, which cannot be discovered by preconceived means only. Greater value is put on spontaneous finding than on premeditative making. The development of Matisse's work is exemplary within this context, embodying the idea that technique stems from the temperament of the artist, and since it reacts anew to new demands it is unstable.

'I do not repudiate any of my paintings,' Matisse says in *Notes of a Painter*, 'yet there is not one I would not paint otherwise if I had to do it over again.' He was guided by his sincerity. Later in life he insisted that it was his only strength.

There are serious problems for us with these notions. If an artist believes that the search for an original discovery is the purpose of art, then that artist must be able to engage a technique which will enable the journey to be made again and again at will, and which, just as crucially, enables him or her to represent originality as if it was a model in itself in the same way as it was an aim.

Matisse, in *Notes of a Painter,* does indicate how this can be achieved by a mixture of initial openness, recognition and exceptional control. But the artist can also devise new technical procedures which subvert conventional methods which have gone stale, and do this deliberately in order to facilitate unforeseen discovery. There are scores of first-hand accounts of this process by artists and by those who have watched them at work. They have become the stock in trade of the modernist artist. T.J. Clark calls them 'practices of negation' ranging from 'The Fauves mismatching of colour on canvas with colour in the world out there' to 'the use of degenerate trivial or inartistic materials', to 'the parodying of previous powerful styles.'

This leads straight on to problems of critical evaluation. How do we identify originality in the deeper sense of being authentic as well as merely different, and not be deceived by its imitation becoming conventional? The critic is simply led to affirm or deny the presence of originality, and greatness too, because if this is the dominant theory then the artist who succeeds in it is the best. Reasoned analysis of meaning via the antecedents or referents of the work becomes moot with regard to qualities presumed to be felt by both artist and viewer. We are back to Greenberg again, with his unprejudiced immediate encounter – all alone with himself.

But the process of artistic expression is today still seen as a means of finding something – possibly oneself. This implies that there is a self which we have lost, or of which we were robbed, by our times or our parents, or by our education or, paradoxically, by another part of ourselves. However, the idea of the unconscious as the site of the natural and the primitive partly loses its power if it is seen to be structured like a language, and witnessed through language. The notion of the artist as the only origin of the work and the critic as the only origin of the criticism becomes as implausible as we knew it would. But I would argue that the concept of the unconscious seems as necessary now as it was at the beginning of the century because at both junctures the values it offers, either as origin or antidote, seem equally under threat and equally powerful. For this reason, the artist has shown healthy resistance to being displaced entirely.

I want to finish by looking at what I've outlined in the context of art schools. I believe the dominant ideology in art school practice to be based on the values in the second grouping or tendency I have described, often without any mediating discourse. Of course there are exceptions – individual students and staff more often than whole institutions. This prevalent mode is based on our obsession with the artist's temperament as the origin of technical means. But the techniques and practices of modernist self-expression, whether non-objective or naturalistic, can be taught and so have become conventional. If their original purposes remain unexamined, the practices continue without awareness of their formative context and because they are in a critical vacuum their potency is vastly diminished, if not actually destroyed. They cease to become practices at all in the true sense because they cannot be re-invented. Of course the range of models in the first tendency I described as emanating from Duchamp is present too, but it is a minority voice in the art school even though this is not the case in art practice generally. It has its problems too, maybe resulting from its love affair with meaning. But that may only look the way it does because the other group seems so unconcerned with meanings and contexts once it leaves the terms of the work itself.

This situation will go on as long as the gulf between theory and practice continues, that gulf which Christopher Frayling described, at the first Wimbledon School of Art conference, as actually programmed into higher education in art thirty years ago.

Students will leave colleges with what look like impressive practices, as I did from the Central and Chelsea at the end of the 1960s, and may achieve success only to find that they don't know what they're doing. There is an argument which says it's inevitable. But I don't accept that. It is deeply depressing. If one side of the equation is missing there's no possibility of a dialectic or evaluation, or much progress. That's why Greenbergian formalism filtered through English educational reticence is such a deadly dead end.

These things are a concern for the whole art school – not just one part of it. Given a little distance we can see that all those intensely individual students are not actually as different from one another as they seemed to be in the maze of their studio spaces. Would it not be better to group students according to specific aspects of art practice and focus our in-depth search on that aspect of practice rather than on an in-depth search of the student? In this way at least there would be an intensification of the act of evaluating because one would have made for them an arena for close attention and for the sharing and refining of values. In theoretical terms too, were theory a living entity in the studios at all, a much more realistic focus would be provided. Instead of going off to do history or theory at the safe and false distance of the seminar room, smaller more realistic subject-specific work could take place. And when will a history and theory course be entirely predicated in its contents and methodology on the fact that the aspiration of those it addresses is to make art? That's why they came to art school in the first place.

As the potential of the student for artistic individuality has increased in importance, so the full potential of the artist-teacher in the art school has diminished. At the moment most of those teachers are expected to consult on any approach, be they in a working relationship with it in their practice or not. This could stimulate productive debate but generally it doesn't, at least not in front of the students. If the artist and the writer about art came into the art school and didn't leave their practice at the door, the values and judgements being used and the questions being asked outside the art school might stand more of a chance of being used and asked inside. This might put the artist under pressure, but the artist is in the art school for art, not primarily for education, and that pressure was once seen as creatively productive for staff and students alike. Otherwise we'll just go on as we are with the values and critical judgements we use in our professional life largely hidden from our students.

In a most regrettable and unintended way, this mimics the commercial art world where it is a priority to suppress certain critical debates and support others in order to maintain the exclusivity so necessary for business. The art school has to be the complete opposite of this and uphold the value of the most open exposition of the subject it can possibly sustain.

Evaluating the content of art teaching

RACHEL MASON

Centre for Post-graduate Teacher Eduction, Leicester Polythecnic

I want to begin by defining evaluation as an activity concerned with appraising the value of some object or process that is carried out by connoisseurs of the object or process being appraised.[1] I shall go on to remind you that this activity is integral to education and that the objects and processes subjected to appraisal vary according to the functions and purposes for which evaluation is being used.

Some Functions of Educational Evaluation

Some functions of evaluation in art and design education are to:
- (i) assess the extent to which students have achieved particular programme goals. (As I am a teacher trainer, I am expected to instruct my students as to how to plan educational objectives as targets to which educational efforts can be directed in addition to assessing their achievements on a Postgraduate Certificate in Education (PGCE) course);
- (ii) diagnose students' strengths and weaknesses with a view to making pedagogical decisions as to what should be done next;
- (iii) determine whether or not students should gain access to art educational opportunities – in 'A' level examinations and interviews for higher education for example;
- (iv) assess the overall quality of art and design programmes – in school curriculum reviews and in validation exercises in higher education for example.

Evaluation of Teaching

Evaluation of teaching performance is central to my professional role as a teacher trainer. A large part of my job is and always has been taken up with visiting schools to observe student-teachers practising teaching in classrooms. Evaluation in this situation is used as an educational medium. The qualitative judgements or statements of value I communicate to student-teachers arising out of my observations of their lessons in progress supply feedback which is aimed at helping them to improve the quality of their teaching as a whole.

Aspects of teaching performance typically commented on include the following:

- (i) Lesson preparation. Routine questions I ask myself are, 'Is the purpose of this lesson clear?' 'Are the instructional details well thought through?'
- (ii) Organisation of art/design equipment/materials. 'Was the correct quantity and type of material made ready in advance?' 'Are safety aspects being

considered? 'Is there a system for storing art work which student-teachers and pupils understand?'

(iii) Communication. 'Is their communication with pupils effective, both on a one-to-one basis and to the class as a whole?'

(iv) Classroom management. 'Is the timing of the various parts of the lesson appropriate?' 'Is there enough time to clear up?'

(v) Discipline. 'Are pupils clear about what is/is not appropriate behaviour in the art room?' 'Are they motivated?'

(vi) Resources. 'Is the student-teacher making good use of relevant resource materials and visual aids?

But judgements of teaching performance cannot be isolated from considerations of curriculum content. It is important to note that art and design curriculum content is something over which I, as a teacher trainer, have little control. Specialist PGCE teacher education courses last a mere thirty-six weeks. Prior to this, student-teachers spend three to four years studying art and design at BA degree level. The assumption must be that BA degree courses provide them with subject training while PGCE courses prepare them to teach.

But what kinds of art and design skills, knowledge, understanding, values and attitudes do they bring to PGCE courses?

My Subject Training in Art

I hope you will forgive me for reminiscing about my own subject training at this point. Before I do, I should tell you that my socialisation into the professional world of fine art was via the National Diploma in Design (NDD) and the two artist-teachers entrusted with this socialisation process in my chosen medium (painting) were Euan Euglow and Norman Adams.

While the emphasis throughout my subject training as a whole was almost exclusively on art production, I do not remember that my two artist-teachers ever once demonstrated painting skills or techniques. Those I now possess, I acquired myself in response to their stringent (and violently conflicting) criticism of my stumbling efforts in the studio. The knowledge of artists and art and history they offered me tended to be biographical and restricted to their personal favourites. How they judged art remained a mystery. Extensive detective work was necessary to determine what criteria they used to assess artistic achievement studying their own art and, in particular, that of other students who received more favourable comments. Because their judgements of artistic excellence appeared diametrically opposed, it became clear that my survival depended on a choice of allegiance to one or other of these 'superheroes'.

The values and beliefs about art I acquired as a consequence of becoming Norman Adams's 'disciple' included the following:

(i) Art is a serious business which has spiritual/religious significance.

(ii) The act of artistic creation is mysterious and irrational; artists do not have control over their own artistic ideas.

[84]

(iii) Nature, particularly landscape, is indispensable to art. An artist's 'visionary perception of nature' can transcend the boundaries of ordinary human consciousness.

(iv) The organising principle for all great art is myth and the Bible is the greatest work of art.

Many will recognise this as a peculiarly British interpretation of artistic reality which owes a great deal to William Blake, and persists to this day, firmly located within a Western European Romantic artistic tradition. But my own Romantic knowledge and understanding of art was assimilated indirectly in person-to-person contact in an informal learning situation (the studio) that was highly charged affectively. It was expressed dogmatically by a teacher who afforded personal experience and emotion priority over intellect. Because this learning was tacit rather than explicit I was unable to recognise it for what it was at that time.[2]

I exorcised my Romantic religious value orientation fifteen years later having carried out a full-scale critical interpretation of Norman Adams's life and work.[3] Once I had explicated his Romantic viewpoint I was able to reflect on its influence on my own ideas and test it against critical discourse in art and art education literature. Only then was I able fully to comprehend that aesthetics and religion are not necessarily inseparable and that fine art can express an artist's vision of all manner of values.

National Curriculum Programmes of Study of Art

Let us look at two 'end of key stage statements' for Knowledge and Understanding of Art in the new National Curriculum, together with suggested programmes of study and examples.[4]

Example 1:

END OF STAGE STATEMENT. By the end of key stage 2 pupils should have demonstrated that they can: recognise the influences of different cultures and contexts and apply a developing knowledge of art.
PROGRAMME OF STUDY. Pupils should: recognise that there are different kinds of art made for different purposes.
EXAMPLE. Pupils could: compare the different purposes of familiar visual forms, e.g. postage stamps, posters, television commercials, portraits. Make a list of all the things at home which they consider to be examples of art and discuss their findings with their teacher and peers.

Example 2:

END OF KEY STAGE ATTAINMENT. By the end of key stage 3 pupils should have demonstrated that they can: evaluate the work of artists, recognising that images, symbols and objects are influenced by diverse cultural and social conditions.
PROGRAMME OF STUDY. Pupils should analyse the work of artists and understand the main codes and conventions they use to convey meaning.

EXAMPLE: Pupils could: recognise and value representations of similar forms in different cultures; e.g. the kite in Chinese, Japanese, Indian and European traditions: compare the wall paintings of muralists working in differing cultures, e.g. Giotto, Diego Rivera; compare the ways that letters and symbols have been used to convey information and ideas in graphic form in different cultures e.g. Egyptian hieroglyphics, Islamic calligraphy, Chinese characters, Bauhaus designers.

Literacy in the Visual Arts

The majority of student teachers accepted on PGCE (Art and Design) Teacher Education courses do not and never have had sufficient breadth – or depth – of knowledge of their subject to implement the above kinds of learning.

The way my art education colleagues at Leicester Polytechnic tackle this problem is by allocating one third of the course contact time out of school (PGCE students are required to spend 60 per cent of course time in schools) to dealing with art and design curriculum content. This is effected in a programme of studies called *Literacy in the Visual Arts* (App.1).

In *Literacy in the Visual Arts*, recognition is afforded the fact that student-teachers are an important learning resource for each other in that their BA Art and Design specialisms are many and varied (furniture design, painting, textiles, product design, fashion, interior design, art history, etc.).

My colleagues begin by providing them with a critical strategy (a formula for talking about art and design in general) which is relatively easy to assimilate[5] and by introducing them to four explanations of art derived from Western aesthetic theory (formalist, imitationist, emotionalist and functionalist). They get them to talk about their BA degree work to each other using the critical strategy and applying the theories.

Secondly, student-teachers explore the range of understandings art historians, philosophers, sociologists, anthropologists and psychologists bring to bear on their subject. Thirdly, they investigate a variety of roles for art in contemporary society with particular reference to mass-media (television, advertising and film) and new technologies, including computers. By way of an assessed course task, student-teachers are required to produce an exhibit which 'illustrates a way in which art and design helps to shape ideas, influence behaviour and/or enriches or gives meaning to peoples lives in contemporary society' (App.2).

The majority of student-teachers on the PGCE course at Leicester appear extremely appreciative of this component of their teacher education programme.

Competencies in Art

Appendix 3 shows a list of competencies in visual arts included in some guidelines for assessing student-teachers' subject matter knowledge and understanding in the United States. The list was compiled by a consortium of professors of art and art education, teachers and school administrators with a view to providing a common framework for assessment across California State University's nineteen campuses.

It is important to note that:

(i)   The subject matter competencies are in line with the so-called Discipline Based Art Education (DBAE) philosophy of art education currently being promoted by the Getty Foundation in the United States.[6] It is considerably more ambitious than our National Curriculum in that it draws from four broad areas of competence in art – namely, art production, art history, art criticism and aesthetics;

(ii) the list refers to the 'what' of evaluation but the document also contains discussion of assessment methods (the 'how');

(iii) the guidelines stress the importance of applying the competencies in both formative and summative evaluation situations in all the university's art and design courses not just in art teacher training.

I do not believe that a competency approach to curriculum planning and evaluation could in itself improve the quality of art teaching and learning in British schools. The important thing about the California list, however, is that it represents a consensus opinion as to what it means to be fully 'educated in art'.[7]

As a teacher trainer, I am singularly unimpressed by the argument that art cannot be evaluated. I remain equally convinced that connoisseurship and evaluation go hand in hand. Some positive outcomes of applying the competency approach in evaluation, however, are that it makes the aims and objectives of programmes public, gives students clearer targets of achievement and provides explicit evidence as to why they are successful or fail. The inadequacy of subject training in art and design as it is currently effected with reference to delivery of the new National Curriculum, is a matter which everyone teaching it at BA Art and Design degree level has to address right now. If the Secretary of State has his way, specialist PGCE courses, together with their Literacy in the Visual Arts components like the one I have presented to you here, will shortly disappear.

Notes

1. In discussing the connoisseurship model of educational evaluation, Eisner argues that judgements about quality have to be carried out by people with a trained perception and experience in the field concerned (connoisseurs); and that appraisal should be holistic (E. Eisner, 'Evaluating the Teaching of Art', unpublished paper, Stanford University 1990.

2. Berger and Luckman describe society as presenting candidates for socialisation with 'significant others' or socialising personnel whose subjective realities or worlds are taken for granted and interiorised (P. Berger and T. Luckman, *The Social Construction of Reality*, Harmondsworth, 1984).

3. R. Mason, 'A Romantic Religious Reality', *Journal of Art and Design Education*, vol.13, no.1, 1984, pp.71–82.

4. *National Curriculum Council Consultative Report: Art*, York 1992.

5. Edmund Feldman's strategy was outlined in his seminal book *Becoming Human through Art*, Englewood Cliffs, 1970. The strategy has four stages, Description, Analysis, Interpretation and Evaluation.

6. Getty Centre for Education in the Arts, *Beyond Creating: The Place for Art in America's Schools*, Los Angeles 1985.

7. According to Eisner (1990, p.12) a competency approach to evaluation assumes the existence of absolute standards and one best method. Given this view, it makes sense to dimensionalise teaching and prescribe possible criteria through which teaching performance can be appraised.

Appendix 1: PGCE Art and Design Education Course Outline – Literacy in the Visual Arts, Centre for Postgraduate Teacher Education, De Montfort University (formerly Leicester Polytechnic)

CENTRE FOR POST GRADUATE TEACHER EDUCATION DE MONTFORT UNIVERSITY (formerly LEICESTER POLYTECHNIC)

PGCE (Art and Design Education) Course
LITERACY IN THE VISUAL ARTS AND DESIGN UNIT

Literacy in the Visual Arts and Design is concerned with the meaning of art and design and particularly, but not exclusively, with the role that language can play in rendering instances of art and design comprehensible – at *varying* levels of understanding and complexity.

Student-teachers on the PGCE Course need to develop their understanding of the subject. This need arises despite their having completed studies in art and design up to degree level at least and, in some cases, having experience in art/design related industry and commerce. Such studies and experience are invariably *highly specialised* in nature and, as a consequence, student-teachers' understanding is narrower than the concerns of *art and design education.*

The terms 'art' and 'design' have a fascinating history of varying uses or applications. However, for the purposes of the course, 'art and design' are taken to be closely related concepts between which the *relationship* is considered to be more significant than the *separation.* The concepts refer to those products and other manifestations of visual form which emanate from the diversity of practices relating to fine art, graphic and industrial design, fashion and textile design, crafts, design and technology, computer generated art and design, mass media, architecture and so forth. Art and design are considered in terms of their relationship on the grounds that there are shared and certain unifying characteristics among the constituent areas or disciplines. It is assumed that the variety of forms not only constitutes the field but also that the recognition and understanding of the essential relatedness comprising this field is prerequisite to a coherent understanding of any of the constituents.

A significant dimension to the meaning of 'art and design', as understood for the purposes of the Course, is that it is a manifestation of culture, and therefore is as diverse in form and meaning as there are cultures in existence. Art and design then, are accepted as being multicultural by definition and their multicultural natures as being manifested in the products and practices of the range of ethnic groups constituting contemporary society.

The *Literacy in the Visual Arts and Design Unit* is designed to extend student-teachers' concepts of art and design, to develop their abilities to respond to works of art and design – particularly through language – and to enhance their understanding of the meaning and significance of art and design in contemporary cultures.

Colin Brookes and Don Hutson – Senior Lecturers in Art and Design Education.

Appendix 2: Course Task – Literacy in the Visual Arts, Centre for Postgraduate Teacher Education, Leicester Polytechnic

DE MONTFORT UNIVERSITY SCHOOL OF ARTS
CENTRE FOR POST GRADUATE TEACHER EDUCATION

PGCE (Art and Design Education) Course 1991–92
COURSE TASK 3 LVA PRESENTATION

1. Introduction

1.1 Our apprehension and appreciation of art and design works are effectively communicated and considerably enhanced through the medium of language. For teachers and students, then, the use of language in encounters with art and design is of considerable importance for understanding. Furthermore, 'Understanding' is an 'attainment target' in the National Curriculum Proposals for Art.

1.2 The descriptive, analytical and interpretive phases of appraisal, seminally considered by Feldman (1970) and Smith (1968), and variously developed since, provide a way in which language convincingly enriches our experience of art and design as spectators and practitioners; as well as teachers and students.

1.3 Various kinds of knowledge, such as that established by the history, sociology, anthropology and philosophy of art and design are necessary and valuable in teaching. Yet there are no *definitive* interpretations of art and design works and the application of phases initially identified by Feldman and Smith, in first and subsequent encounters with them can be worthwhile and revealing. Knowing little, or even nothing about a work, or never having seen it before, does not mean that one can say nothing sensitive, discerning and intelligent about it.

1.4 During the first term in LVA seminars, the phases referred to above were considered in their application to your art and design works. It was intended to help extend your capacities to speak spontaneously and unselfconsciously about art and design works in clear, interesting and coherent ways. Talk about art and design was linked to and informed by references to major theories and properties of art and design discussed in the LVA Reader.

2. Course Task

2.1 During the Spring term, you will be required to describe, analyse and interpret a work of a work of art and design. In doing so you will need to attend to those properties identified in the LVA Reader, as these are inherent in the work. The task will take the form of a limited and selective presentation to your LVA group and tutor. The time available for your presentation will be approximately *fifteen* minutes.

2.2 The work in question is to be chosen and provided by yourself. Originals are preferable if this is not possible, then a reproduction of adequate size and quality should be made available for your presentation. The instance of art or design that you select is not to be one of your own, nor one of your colleague's that has been discussed during the LVA sessions this term. The work may or may not be well known to you and it is important to stress that this does not matter – sometimes familiarity can be disadvantageous in that it can make one 'blind' to certain features or works, or assume them to be present just because an 'authority' says so. While some relevant contextual information will have to be sought to provide a coherent reading of the work, prior knowledge will *not*, in itself, form a criterion for assessment. If you wish, you may refer to prepared notes during your presentation but it must be emphasised that in no way are you expected to read a paper – *on the contrary, you will be expected to engage in 'dialogue' with the work of your choice.*

3. Criteria for Assessment

Assessment will focus on the dialogue with the chosen work and the criteria emphasise:
3.1 appropriateness in the use of relevant contextual information;
3.2 the sensitivity, perceptiveness and clarity of articulation in the dialogue with respect to properties identified in the LVA Reader – mimetic, formal, emotional/expressive and functional;
3.3 the persuasiveness and coherence of the descriptive, analytical and interpretative phrases in relation to the work;
3.4 the appropriateness of emphasis given to phrases and properties in relation to the work.

The nature of the Course Task and the criteria for assessment should make it clear that the assignment draws on the LVA seminar work of the first term.

4. Where any item of equipment is required from the Centre to display the selected work, *you must let LVA staff know at least one week prior to your scheduled presentation.* A timetable for the organisation of presentations will be drawn by your seminar tutor.

5. If you are unclear about any part of this Course Task, you should seek clarification from staff well before your presentation; there should be no doubt in your mind as to what is required of you.

Appendix 3: List of Competencies in Visual Arts Used for Assessment at California State University

	METHODS OF ASSESSMENT OF COMPETENCIES OF PROSPECTIVE ART TEACHERS - FRESNO CAMPUS									
		METHODS OF ASSESSMENT								
	COMPETENCIES	Waiver Program	Classroom Studio Activities	Interview	Portfolio	Campus Test	Campus Essay	NTE Score	Grade Point Average	Capstone Course	Other
1	Understands relationship between Components	X	X	X						X	
2	Can Intellectualise about Art	X	X	X						X	
3	Can relate Art, Thinking and Learning	X	X	X						X	
4	Understands Art is Essential Human Activity	X	X	X						X	
5	Understands Art Reflects Society	X	X	X						X	
6	Understands Relevance of Art	X	X	X						X	
7	Awareness of California Arts Framework		X	X							
8	Is Competent in at Least Two Art Media	X	X	X	X				X		
9	Has Range of Art Media Competencies	X	X	X	X						
10	Can Choose Themes/Ideas to Create Art Works	X	X	X	X						
11	Can Describe Own "Creative" Process	X	X	X							
12	Can Discuss Expressive Qualities of Media	X	X	X						X	
13	Can Describe & Imitate Styles of Artworks	X	X	X						X	
14	Can Evaluate Works of Self and Peers	X	X	X							
15	Can Describe Formal Elements in an Artwork	X	X	X						X	
16	Understands Developmental Acquisition of Skills		X	X							
17	Sees Art Heritage with Conprehensive View	X	X	X						X	
18	Understands Role of Art in Value Formation	X	X	X						X	
19	Knows Methods for Historical Inquiry in Art	X	X	X						X	
20	Can Use Art to Make Inferences about Future	X	X	X						X	
21	Appreciates Contributions of Diverse Groups	X	X	X						X	X
22	Understands how Art Functions Culturally	X	X	X						X	X
23	Can Write "Critically" about Works of Art	X	X	X						X	
24	Can Interpret Meaning in Works of Art	X	X	X						X	
25	Can Find and Identify Works of Art Criticism	X	X	X						X	
26	Understands how Perspective Affects Meaning	X	X	X						X	X
27	Knows how to Assess and Communicate Judgements	X	X	X						X	
28	Knows where Significant Art Works are Found	X	X	X						X	
29	Understands how "Art Criticism" is Developmed	X	X	X						X	
30	Can Articulate Personal Philosophy of Art	X	X	X						X	
31	Can Discuss Work of Major Philosophers of Art	X	X	X						X	
32	Can Apply Critical and Logical Processes to Art	X	X	X						X	
33	Appreciates Multiple Aesthetic Values	X	X	X						X	
34	Understands How Philosophical Inquiry Develops	X	X	X						X	